"This book is a gift. I didn't realize how much I didn't know how to pray for my children until I held it in my hands! With wisdom and love, James Banks equips parents to *love our children* through prayer."

—Margot Starbuck,
author of *The Girl in the Orange Dress*

"Nothing moves the heart of a parent more than the need of a child. Nothing moves the heart of God more than the cry of His children. Nothing ignites powerful prayer more than the truths of God's Word. That's why I love this book. My friend, James Banks, is a father who has prayed in earnest for his children and found his heavenly Father's heart in the pages of the Word of God. Join him in this ninety-day journey of prayer that will undoubtedly be instructive, authentic, and truly inspiring."

—Daniel Henderson,
President, Strategic Renewal

"In *Prayers for Your Children*, James Banks lays out a simple plan for how to combine combustible elements—the power of God's Word, your faith in the Father, and your love for your children—so that prayer emerges as an explosive force that nothing can avert. Prayer can release the power of God into the cracks and crevices of a heart when nothing else can penetrate. Prayer can search out and disarm life's land mines before they detonate. Nothing is beyond prayer's powerful reach. This book will give you a practical plan for how you can discover fresh power in prayer for the lives of your children."

ennedy Dean, Executive Director of
The Praying Life Foundation and
author of *Live a Praying Life*

"James Banks writes from the heart of a father who knows what it's like to pray for a prodigal to return home. From praying for your children to discover the power of prayer, to asking the Lord to give them faith that surpasses your own—James uses the power of Scripture to help you pray toward their eternal destinies. By using this book as a guide, you will not run out of kingdom prayers for your children."

—Carol Madison, editor of *Prayer Connect* magazine

"James Banks has written a book that not only helps parents put the power of prayer into action, but will be a great scriptural guide to strengthen their devotional life."

—Chrissy Cymbala Toledo,
author of *The Girl in the Song*

"Thirty-eight years ago the Holy Spirit pressed me to pray every day for our four children. It wasn't easy. There were times, sadly, that I failed. My prayers would have been wider, deeper, and richer had I had this wonderful resource by Dr. James Banks. I thank God for *Prayers for Your Children*. It will enhance and enrich my prayers as I now pray for twelve grandchildren."

—Dr. Alvin Vander Griend, author of eight books on prayer and
Prayer-Evangelism Associate for Harvest Prayer Ministries

"For every concern on behalf of your children, James Banks has beautifully crafted a sincere, tender lifetime resource to help you 'approach the throne of grace with confidence' (Hebrews 4:16)."

—Sarah Bush, blogger and author

Prayers for Your Children

**90 DAYS OF HEARTFELT PRAYERS
FOR CHILDREN OF ANY AGE**

JAMES BANKS

Discovery House
from Our Daily Bread Ministries

Discovery House is affiliated with Our Daily Bread Ministries, Grand Rapids, Michigan.

Requests for permission to quote from this book should be directed to: Permissions Department, Discovery House, P.O. Box 3566, Grand Rapids, MI 49501, or contact us by e-mail at permissionsdept@dhp.org.

Library of Congress Cataloging-in-Publication Data
Banks, James, 1961-
Prayers for your children : 90 days of heartfelt prayers for children of any age / James Banks.
    pages cm
Includes index.
ISBN 978-1-62707-333-2
1. Prayer—Christianity. 2. Prayers. 3. Bible—Prayers. 4. Parents—Religious life. I. Title.
BV210.3.B364 2015
242'.845—dc23

Interior designed by Melissa Elenbaas

Printed in the United States of America
Second printing in 2015

And he took the children in his arms . . .
and blessed them.

Mark 10:16

To Noemi Dotres.

The worth of your prayers will never be
known this side of heaven.

CONTENTS

ACKNOWLEDGMENTS

So many have poured prayer into this book I cannot thank them all. But may I try?

The people of Peace Church in Durham have faithfully encouraged and walked with me step by step, up to the throne of grace and back again. I would rather sit beside you at Jesus' feet than anywhere else.

Faithful readers and friends—many of whom I haven't met (*yet*)—have loved me and my family with your prayers as if we were your own. I look forward to one day looking back with you at all that your prayers have won. And it is already much.

Miranda Gardner and Paul Muckley, how blessed I am to have such skillful (and patient and faithful) editors who run to the Father as you work. His creativity, love, and attention to detail move through you to reach others in immeasurable, beautiful ways.

For the larger team at Discovery House Publishers and Our Daily Bread Ministries: Mart DeHaan, Carol Holquist, Judy Markham, John van der Veen, Denise Grubb, Tim Jackson, Dennis Moles, Ed Rock, Katy Pent, Anne Bauman, Ruth Watson, Amy Wenger-Cerra, and so many others. . . . Your refreshing vision for books that reach people for eternal purposes makes working with you the privilege of a lifetime.

So many friends along the way . . . Howard and Margaret Shockley, Dick and Shirilee Little, John Holecek, Daniel and Jordan Henderson, Joel Collier, Don Westbrook, Dub Karriker, Gary Stewart, Garth Rosell, Bob Mayer, Bill Enns, Ken Priddy, Lindy Apon, Bob and Jane Plapp, Chris Greenwood, David Beaty, Andy Traub, John Blake, Marty Duffell, David McClean, Gary McGhee, Katie Krieger, Allen and Cathleen Huff. . . . Heaven has heard you more than once on my behalf!

Stef and Geoff, this book couldn't have been written without you. I'm so thankful to be your dad. Thank you for your courage in letting me share some of your stories.

Cari, you have once again lived up to the meaning of your name (*Cari* is short for *Caridad*, which means "Charity"). Your faithfulness in daily life together and in consistent prayer for your husband and children is a priceless gift from God.

It is for the Gift above all gifts, the One who is at the right hand of the Father "pleading for us" (Romans 8:34 NLT), that this book has been written. I would be lost without His love. Beautiful Savior, I pray these prayers may be used to bring you the "praise and honor and glory" (Revelation 5:13) that you deserve forever!

INTRODUCTION

Prayers to Love By

> My dear mother, besides the pains she
> took with me, often commended me
> with many prayers and tears to God, and
> I doubt not but I reap the fruits of these
> prayers to this hour.
>
> John Newton

One of the best ways we can love our children is by praying for them.

God waits for us to pray so He can bring good into their lives that would not have happened any other way. He loves to answer prayer, and when we pray with even a little faith, we open the door to what only He can do. No matter what their age or accomplishments, our children always need us to pray.

The overwhelming response to my book *Prayers for Prodigals* made clear that there was a need for another book that would encourage moms and dads to pray more for *any* son or daughter with the powerful promises God has given us. Parents know they need to pray, but sometimes it's easy to stay "stuck" in our own thoughts, ideas, and desires for our kids. We need the fresh inspiration of God's Spirit to fill our minds and hearts and lift us to new places of grace.

You might think of the prayers in this book as a launching pad for your own. The real fuel in them is God's Word, and there's no limit to where He may take you.

This book contains ninety days of prayers drawn from much-loved passages of Scripture. You'll pray for your son or daughter using "The Love Chapter" (1 Corinthians 13) and the Twenty-Third Psalm. You'll pray through "The Fruit of the Spirit" (Galatians 5:22–23), every piece of "The Armor of God" (Ephesians 6:11–18) and several other powerful passages for personal and spiritual growth. Each section begins with a brief reflection introducing the week's theme, a biblical concept helpful for living the Christian faith. The thirteen themes are Knowing, Growing, Walking, Loving, Protected, Faithful, Fruitful, Thankful, Humble, Pure, Hopeful, Overcoming, and Blessed.

All of the prayers emphasize the importance of a loving and practical relationship with God through Jesus Christ. There are an equal number of prayers for sons and daughters of any age, and you can easily adapt them by switching the pronouns ("he" or "she") as needed. This book is also designed so that you will keep praying after you've finished reading—that's why most of the prayers don't end with an "amen." And there is space at the conclusion of every prayer for you to add your own thoughts and notes as you continue to lift up your child in Jesus' name.

God blesses Christian parents with children so that we *will* pray for them. Our children are a sacred trust; they've been given to us for eternal purposes so that we might point them to our Savior. Can we ever pray too much? The full impact of our prayers for our children's salvation and every other "good and perfect gift" (James 1:17) in their lives will never be known this side of heaven. But we *do know* we are to "pray continually" (1 Thessalonians 5:17), as we carry out our responsibility to "bring them up in the training and instruction of the Lord" (Ephesians 6:4). We need to pray not only when there are problems in their lives; we should go to God so that their best days can be better and every day can be lifted and blessed. We have a God-given responsibility to pray for them as long as we live. And we have the comfort of knowing that because of God's kindness our prayers can even outlive us, finding their answers years after our own lives on this earth are done.

Who can pray for your son or daughter like you can? It's not about the words you use. It's about God's faithfulness, and your heart as a mom or dad. There's incredible power in a parent's prayers—the power of *"Abba*, Father" (Mark 14:36), who allows himself be moved by our heartfelt prayers in beautiful ways. He knows and loves our children even more than we do! Our goal when we pray is simply to bring our kids to Jesus for His help and blessing on every circumstance of their lives. They're better off in His hands than in our own.

> Now to him who is able to do immeasurably more than all we ask or imagine, according to his power that is at work within us, to him be glory in the church and in Christ Jesus throughout all generations, for ever and ever! Amen.
>
> Ephesians 3:20–21

Week 1

KNOWING

Mom's Gift

> I keep asking that the God of our Lord
> Jesus Christ, the glorious Father, may give
> you the Spirit of wisdom and revelation,
> so that you may know him better.
>
> Ephesians 1:17

"God has something for you to do. I just know it. . . ."

Those words from my mom stuck with me. But it would be years before I would take them to heart.

Sometimes believing moms have a way of "knowing" things that are known only to God. I don't know why that is, but I've learned it from personal experience. And it all started with a wreck.

When Mom was pregnant with me, she had a car accident on a winding mountain road in Southern California. She lost control of her 1958 Pontiac Super Chief on a steep downhill curve without guardrails. The car veered off the road and narrowly missed rolling into the canyon below.

Al, the tow truck driver called to the scene, was a friend of the family. His service station was just down Main Street from my parents' store. "I don't know why you didn't go into that canyon," he told Mom. "The tire tracks say you shouldn't be here right now. Someone was looking out for you."

Mom never forgot that. She didn't let *me* forget it either. And the way she always put it was, "God has something for you to do. . . ."

Every time something of significance happened in my life, she would remind me. Whenever I doubted what I believed or was discouraged, she'd make the point again. Like Beethoven's Fifth, she wove the same theme over and over again throughout my young life. It was her symphony, a magnum opus straight from her soul.

Each time that Mom pointed me to God she was giving me a gift. But I didn't know it then. More than once when I was a teenager I would walk into the room in the middle of the day and find her sitting in a chair with her eyes closed . . .

"Wake up, Mom."

She opened one eye and raised an eyebrow.

"I *am* awake. I'm praying. Praying for *you*."

Mom's heartfelt desire was for each of her children to get close enough to God so they could discover what she already knew. He could fill our lives with meaning and purpose that could be found nowhere else. Looking back, I'm convinced that her prayers kept me out of the bottom of more than one canyon.

A parent's prayers can summon angels. But God can use them for even more. It was Augustine who prayed, "You made us for yourself, and our hearts are restless until they rest in you."[1] The prayers in the pages that follow are intended to point our sons and daughters to what Jesus alone can give them. What could give them more peace, joy, and fulfillment than knowing Him? Or as Jesus himself put it, "What do you benefit if you gain the whole world but lose your own soul?" (Mark 8:36 NLT).

There is only one "author of life" (Acts 3:15), and only He knows how our stories were meant be written. He alone can save us from our sins and ourselves and inspire our lives with eternal purpose. With Him, each new chapter holds fresh hope and promise, and the end on this earth is only the beginning. "No eye has seen, no ear has heard, and no mind has imagined what God has prepared for those who love him" (1 Corinthians 2:9–10 NLT).

When we pray for our children to know Jesus we leave them a legacy of love. What better gift could we give our children than our passionate prayers for their salvation?

---

1. Augustine of Hippo. *The Confessions of St. Augustine.* Translated by Rex War-
    ner. New Kensington, PA: Whitaker House, 1996, p. 11.

BORN TO YOU!

Indeed, of Zion it will be said, "This one
and that one were born in her,
and the Most High himself will establish
her." The LORD will write
in the register of the peoples: "This one
was born in Zion."
As they make music they will sing, "All my
fountains are in you."

Psalm 87:5–7

I remember when I first held her in my arms. What a miracle!

Beautiful bright eyes and a rosebud mouth. A living, breathing gift from you.

When I recall how precious she was to me in that moment, it makes me think about you.

How much does it mean to you, Father, when we are "born again" (John 3:3)?

I can only begin to imagine. If I multiply the love I felt at my daughter's birth a thousand times over, I'm barely scratching the surface of the joy you, the unlimited

"Everlasting God" (Genesis 21:33[a]) and "author of life" (Acts 3:15), must feel each time a living soul turns to you from sin.

Lord Jesus, you said "There is . . . joy in heaven over one lost sinner who repents" (Luke 15:7[b])!

What joy must fill your heart when we are "born of the Spirit" (John 3:6[c])! So today I pray my daughter will bring you joy. I pray for her salvation.

By faith I can see her as you hold her in your arms and the angels gather round for a closer look.

May it be said of her, "This one was born in Zion" (Psalm 87:6)!

How could anything compare "with the infinite value of knowing" (Philippians 3:8[d]) you as Savior?

Let her know the wonder of the limitless life you give, because your Spirit lives within her and her body is "a temple" set apart for you (1 Corinthians 6:19[e]).

May she give herself to you because you "bought" her "with a high price" through your death on the cross (1 Corinthians 6:20[f]).

May she drink deeply from you, "the spring of living water" (Jeremiah 2:13) and "never thirst" again (John 4:14[g])!

I pray she will come to understand it is by your kindness and grace she has been "saved through faith," and this is not her "own doing"—it is a priceless gift from you (Ephesians 2:8[h]).

Lord Jesus, I ask that she will "work hard" to live for you above all things so that she may "never fall away" (2 Peter 1:10[i]) and "will receive a rich welcome" into your "kingdom that lasts forever" (2 Peter 1:11[j]).

I praise you, Father, because you are "more powerful than anyone else," and "no one can snatch" us out of your hand (John 10:29[k]).

May her name be written in your "book of life" (Revelation 20:12)!

May she know your promise to be true in her heart: "Fear not, for I have redeemed you; I have called you by name, you are mine" (Isaiah 43:1[l]).

"How great is the love" (1 John 3:1[m]) you have "lavished on us, that we should be called" your children (1 John 3:1)! I pray she will be yours forever!

a ESV, b NLT, c ESV, d NLT, e ESV, f NLT, g NKJV, h ESV, i NLT, j NIrV, k NLT, l ESV, m NIrV

DECLARING DEPENDENCE

"As for me, far be it from me that I should sin against the LORD by failing to pray for you."

1 Samuel 12:23

Father, please help me to remember Samuel's words to your people and take them to heart.

I don't want to sin against you by "failing to pray" for my child (1 Samuel 12:23)!

I know you want me to pray, and I know my child needs me to.

You have given him to me so that I might pray for him and raise him to believe in you and know you.

If I don't pray for him, who will?

I want to follow your example in prayer, Lord Jesus.

"During the days" of your "life on earth," you "offered up prayers and petitions with fervent cries and tears" (Hebrews 5:7). Help me to pray with passion too!

You "would *often* slip away to the wilderness and pray" (Luke 5:16ᵃ).

25

If you were entirely "without sin" (Hebrews 4:15[b]) yet felt
the need to pray, I know I need to pray as well!

Thank you for the blessings you give when we pray, Lord.
"You faithfully answer our prayers with awesome deeds,
O God our Savior" (Psalm 65:5[c])!

I don't want my child to miss a single one of the "benefits"
(Psalm 103:2) you so richly pour out on those who love
you and "call upon" your "name" (1 Chronicles 16:8[d]).

I want to set an example for my son in prayer, Lord. Please
give me grace to stay very close to you so that I "never
stop praying" (1 Thessalonians 5:17[e]).

And if he catches me on my knees when I "go into" my
room, "close the door and pray" (Matthew 6:6), may it
be a declaration of dependence on you that he always
remembers!

You open doors when we pray, doors beyond our imagining.

You are "the One who breaks open the way" (Micah 2:13),
and what you open "no one can shut" (Isaiah 22:22).

How kind you are, Father, to give us the privilege of prayer!
What incredible things can be accomplished!

I pray my son will grasp this and walk faithfully with you.

May he learn to pray in such a way that his heart grows
bigger; I ask that he will be so caught up in the wonder
of your love that he takes your interests to heart. Then,
when he discovers the things that you are after, he will
"know that" you hear him (1 John 5:15[f]) and will be
blessed all the more.

May your "face shine upon" him (Numbers 6:25[g]) so that
he sees you move in answer to prayer again and again!

Show him the goodness of all that you are, Lord, so that
he "calls on your name" and "strives to lay hold of you"
(Isaiah 64:7).

"There is none like you, Lord; no deeds can compare with
yours" (Psalm 86:8)!

"What joy for those you choose to bring near" (Psalm 65:4[h]),
who live out their days in your presence in prayer!

a NASB, b NASB, c NLT, d NASB, e NLT, f ESV, g NKJV, h NLT

"YES, JESUS LOVES ME"

> I want to know Christ and experience the Mighty power that raised him from the dead.
>
> Philippians 3:10 (NLT)

'Jesus loves me, this I know, for the Bible tells me so.'

I want my child always to know that you love her, Lord Jesus.

I pray she may know that with all of her heart because you "dwell" in her heart "through faith" (Ephesians 3:17[a]).

You've given your life for her; I pray she will discover the fulfilling adventure that you, "the author of life" (Acts 3:15), long to share with her.

You are "the one who is life itself" (1 John 1:2[b])!

I pray she will have a relationship with you that keeps growing deeper as long as she lives.

May she treat the good news about you "like a treasure" (Matthew 13:44[c]), the most valuable thing in her life!

May she know the beauty of your peace, "which exceeds anything we can understand" (Philippians 4:7[d]).

I pray she will always take comfort in your love because through you our "comfort abounds" (2 Corinthians 1:5) in the most challenging places of our lives, giving fresh strength.

May you be her last thought when she lays her head on a pillow at night and her first thought when she gets up in the morning.

I pray she will "sing and make music" in her heart to you (Ephesians 5:19) as her heart is filled with your loving presence.

May her entire life be filled with your purpose, because apart from you, we "can do nothing" (John 15:5ᵉ).

I pray she will always be assured of your love, so that she may know with all her "heart and soul that not one of all of the good promises" you have given her has failed (Joshua 23:14).

Sometimes I think of myself as someone who gave her life—but in reality, every breath she has is a gift from you.

I pray she will give up herself to you by following you even when it is difficult, turning from herself to you. You have told us that "whoever would save his life will lose it, but whoever loses his life" for your sake "will find it" (Matthew 16:25ᶠ).

May she know you as "the God who answered my prayers" when she needs it most.

May she say of you, "He has been with me wherever I have gone" (Genesis 35:3ᵍ).

When she thinks of heaven, I pray she will think of you most of all!

I ask she may know your "mighty power" that gives life (Philippians 3:10[h]) throughout her years, so that no matter how old she grows, she will always "look forward" to you (2 Peter 3:12)!

a ESV, b NLT, c ESV, d NLT, e ESV, f ESV, g NLT, h NLT

HEART KNOWLEDGE

"When I discovered your words, I
devoured them.
They are my joy and my heart's delight,
for I bear your name,
O Lord God of Heaven's Armies."

Jeremiah 15:16 (NLT)

I pray he will be a man of your Word, Lord.

What better way to know you than by meeting you in your Word?

But I don't just pray for 'head knowledge'—the Pharisees and the Sadducees had that and they didn't recognize you.

I pray for 'heart knowledge.' "Knowledge puffs up while love builds up" (1 Corinthians 8:1).

I pray he will know you personally by discovering you in your Word and falling in love with you there.

I think of some of the moments we've had together in the pages of your Word. It was as if you were in the room with me, sitting right beside me.

Even when I didn't sense your presence in the moment, how often a verse would come back to me later in the day, showing me you were there all along, preparing me for whatever it is I might face.

How you speak to us through your Word, guiding, guarding, and teaching us in our relationship with you.

I ask that you, "the God of our Lord Jesus Christ, the glorious Father," may give my child "the Spirit of wisdom and revelation, so that" he "may know" you better (Ephesians 1:17).

May he long to meet you in the pages of your Word, day after day!

I pray that every day he will have a fresh understanding of how your Word applies to his life.

"All Scripture is God-breathed" (2 Timothy 3:16). I ask that through your Word you breathe life into him through the power of your Spirit!

May he be like a hungry man at a feast, filled and strengthened with every bite of your truth. May your words be his "joy" and his "heart's delight" (Jeremiah 15:16[a]).

I pray he will "listen" to you and "eat what is good." Then he "will enjoy the finest food" (Isaiah 55:2[b]), the sustenance that only comes from you.

Teach him "Your way, O LORD," so he "will walk in Your truth" (Psalm 86:11[c]). Give him "an undivided heart" (Psalm 86:11) so he may honor you in all he does.

"Every word" you speak "proves true"; you are "a shield to all who come" to you for "protection" (Proverbs 30:5[d]).

Please give him grace "to understand what really matters," Lord Jesus, so that he may live a "pure and blameless" life "until the day" of your return (Philippians 1:10ᵉ).

"O Lord, you are a great and awesome God! You always fulfill your covenant and keep your promises of unfailing love to those who love you and obey your commands" (Daniel 9:4ᶠ).

I pray he will love you and love your Word so he may live in your joy forever!

a NLT, b NLT, c NASB, d NLT, e NLT, f NLT

"I'VE GOT YOU!"

For you have delivered my soul from
   death,
my eyes from tears, my feet from
   stumbling;
I will walk before the LORD in the land of
   the living.

Psalm 116:8–9 (ESV)

Skinned knees, bumps and bruises . . .

I haven't always been able to catch my child in time, Lord.

I know I can't always keep her from pain, no matter how much I would like to or how hard I may try.

She is safer in your hands than mine. She is, after all, the work "of Your hands" (Psalm 92:4ᵃ), just like I am. And "you have delivered my soul from death, my eyes from tears," and "my feet from stumbling" (Psalm 116:8ᵇ).

Where would I be without you, Lord Jesus?

What would have happened to me if you didn't hold me "in your hands" (Psalm 31:15)?

You have helped me so many times! There is no better place to be than in your care.

I long for her to hear your Spirit whisper, "Don't be afraid, for I am with you. Don't be discouraged, for I am your God. I will strengthen you and help you. I will hold you up" (Isaiah 41:10[c]).

'I've got you!' That's what I'd tell her when she would trip and fall and I was there to catch her.

That's also what I'd say when she would run and jump into my arms just for the joy of it.

Oh, for her to hear *you* say that! I pray that my daughter will take a leap of faith into your arms!

I pray she will genuinely know you and run to you every day that she lives on this earth.

"Those who know your name trust in you, for you, Lord, have never forsaken those who seek you" (Psalm 9:10).

You are "able to keep" her from "stumbling" and to present her before your "glorious presence without fault and with great joy" (Jude 24)!

Your strong hands, "pierced for our transgressions" (Isaiah 53:5), will catch her every time.

You are "the faithful God." You lavish your "unfailing love on those who love" you and obey you (Deuteronomy 7:9[d]).

I pray she will love and obey you! All the help and comfort I could ever hope to give her would never compare with "the beauty" of your presence (Psalm 27:4) and your Spirit in her, because your "Spirit joins with our spirit to affirm" that we are your "children" (Romans 8:16[e]).

I pray she may know she is yours, and always praise you for it!

a NASB, b ESV, c NLT, d NLT, e NLT

ASKING RIGHT

God said to Solomon, "Because your
    greatest desire is to help your people,
and you did not ask for wealth, riches,
    fame, or even the death of your
    enemies
or a long life, but rather you asked for wis-
    dom and knowledge
to properly govern my people—I will
    certainly give you the wisdom and
    knowledge
you requested. But I will also give you
    wealth, riches, and fame such as
no other king has had before you or will
    ever have in the future!"
2 Chronicles 1:11–12 (NLT)

I'm reminded of how you blessed Solomon when he asked wisely.

You blessed him above and beyond what he expected because his "greatest desire" was to help his people (2 Chronicles 1:11[a]).

He didn't ask for "wealth, riches, fame" for himself. He didn't even ask for "a long life" (2 Chronicles 1:11[b])! He just wanted what was best for someone you cared deeply about. I want to take that example to heart. So today I ask you to bless my child, Lord, knowing that I will be blessed when you do!

You have said you will show "love to a thousand generations of those who love" you (Deuteronomy 5:10).

I do love you, Lord! And I praise you that you want to show your love to my child for generations to come!

You kindly and generously gave him to me, and today I place him in your hands again.

I cannot presume to know all of what is best for him—I need you to show me, so I ask for wisdom in my asking.

I have many thoughts, dreams, and even ambitions for him, Father. Please help me to submit all of them to you and be your servant for my son's salvation.

I ask that you "give" me more of your "Holy Spirit" just as you promised (Luke 11:13), so that I might learn to want what you want for him.

You "know the plans" you have for my child—plans to give him "hope and a future" (Jeremiah 29:11). I can only begin to imagine what you planned for him, with love, even before you "made the world" (Ephesians 1:4[c]).

How wonderful you are! You truly are "the Awesome One" (Psalm 76:11[d])!

Help me always to point my son to you, so that he might seek "your face with all" his heart (Psalm 119:58)!

Lord Jesus, you "called the children" to yourself (Luke 18:16). I pray he will hear you calling and draw near. May he always want to be close to you!

May he "live by faith" in you, "the Son of God," because you love him (Galatians 2:20[e]).

I pray he will live out his days in love with you!

You gave yourself up "for our sins, just as God our Father planned, in order to rescue us from this evil world in which we live" (Galatians 1:4[f]).

Please help him to know what you have rescued him from and be grateful to you for it!

May he "live a life filled with love" (Ephesians 5:2[g]), thankful for your goodness, aware that "you are near" (Psalm 119:151).

"What joy for those who trust in you" (Psalm 84:12[h])! I pray you will always be his joy, so that he may be blessed forever!

a NLT, b NLT, c NLT, d NLT, e ESV, f NLT, g NLT, h NLT

Day 7

WHERE THE WILD THINGS WERE

For you were once darkness, but now you
are light in the Lord. Live as children of
light (for the fruit of the light consists in all
goodness, righteousness and truth) and
find out what pleases the Lord.

Ephesians 5:8–10

Today I pray my child will know the change that only you can make in a life, Father.

How easy it is for us to tell ourselves, 'I've always been this way!' and to wonder if we really can leave old, wild habits of the heart behind.

But you change hearts every day. "Anyone who belongs to Christ has become a new person. The old life is gone; a new life has begun!" (2 Corinthians 5:17[a]).

Real change is possible with you, and I praise you for it!

Where there was once chaos in our lives, you give us your peace. "You have rescued me from death; you have kept my feet from slipping. So now I can walk in your presence, O God, in your life-giving light" (Psalm 56:13[b]).

I thank you that I don't struggle with some of the things I once did. Even though I "stumble in many ways" (James 3:2), you've changed my heart. Deep inside I no longer want the old ways. I want yours!

I pray that my daughter will too. "What counts is the new creation" (Galatians 6:15)! May you live through her with your life-giving power as she gives up her will and her ways to you!

I pray she will come to the place where she can say, "My old self has been crucified with Christ. It is no longer I who live, but Christ lives in me. So I live in this earthly body by trusting in the Son of God, who loved me and gave himself for me" (Galatians 2:20ᶜ).

May she be real with you so that she may know the reality of all that you are!

Keep her from the trap that you warn of in your Word: "These people come near to me with their mouth and honor me with their lips, but their hearts are far from me" (Isaiah 29:13).

Let her be open and honest with you about those places where she struggles with sin so that she may discover how intimately you care for her—and how truly trans-formational your power and love can be!

How good you are, Lord! You delight "in those who fear" you, "who put their hope" in your "unfailing love" (Psalm 147:11).

"Let your face shine" on her, Lord. Save her "in your unfailing love" (Psalm 31:16)!

May she know the soul-satisfying happiness of your smile and say in response: "O LORD, I am your servant; yes, I am your servant . . . you have freed me from my chains" (Psalm 116:16[d]).

May she know the chain-breaking, "glorious liberty of the children of God" (Romans 8:21[e]), who praise you together, saying "Yes, the LORD has done amazing things for us! What joy!" (Psalm 126:3[f]).

a NLT, b NLT, c NLT, d NLT, e NKJV, f NLT

Week 2

GROWING

Marks in God's Doorway

> But grow in the grace and knowledge of
> our Lord and Savior Jesus Christ.
> To him be glory both now and forever!
> Amen.
>
> 2 Peter 3:18

We have a door frame at home that I refuse to paint. I've put a few coats on the room around it several times, but never on the frame. I won't even scrub it. When I clean around the frame, it's with all the care of an archaeologist preserving a priceless artifact. And if we ever move from the house, I'm taking that part of the door frame with me.

Why? Because of several simple lines in ink, each one with a name and date: growth marks placed there for every year of our children's lives.

I put each line there, one by one. Some years they were very close to each other, and then came the growth spurts. But every mark was a milestone.

Looking at that those lines makes me wonder if God does something similar with us, marking the moments and celebrating bursts of growth. . . .

You do the right thing and avoid the wrong because you know if you did otherwise it would "grieve the Holy Spirit" (Ephesians 4:30). God pulls out His pen.

You choose to forgive someone without their having to ask you. God draws a line with an exclamation point!

You sacrifice to serve because you're doing it for Jesus. God marks the moment in red, and stands back and smiles. Every mark matters. Even the lowest line on the doorway fills His heart with love.

Sure, I'm only speculating, and it all sounds so sentimental. But why not? When it comes to growth, we're standing on solid scriptural ground. We are to "grow up" in our "salvation," Peter tells us, once we "have tasted that the Lord is good" (1 Peter 2:2–3). He also reminds us to "grow in the grace and knowledge of our Lord and Savior Jesus Christ" (2 Peter 3:18). Once we are "born again" (1 Peter 1:23), something would be desperately wrong if we didn't keep on growing.

It's not about legalism, it's about love. Jesus said, "If you love me, you will do what I command" (John 14:15 ESV). But no matter how much progress we make, it's always growth in "grace," as Peter put it. We walk in the strength Jesus gives and not our own.

We all have growing to do. In light of eternity, even the most mature believer on this earth is still very young—still standing in God's doorway. And that's where our prayers come in.

Paul wrote the church in Colosse, "Since the day we heard about you, we have not stopped *praying for you. We continually ask God* to fill you with the knowledge of his will through all the wisdom and understanding that the Spirit gives, *so that* you may *live a life worthy of the Lord and please him in every way*: bearing fruit in every good work, *growing* in the knowledge of God, being strengthened with all power according to his glorious might" (Colossians 1:9–11, italics added).

There's a clear connection here between faithful, consistent prayer for others and their growth in grace. Paul and Timothy were praying that the growth of the believers in the Colossian church would put a smile on God's face. That's also what the prayers in these pages are about for our daughters and sons.

God wants our children to keep growing regardless of their age. Adults look at kids with excitement and say, "How you've grown!" Is it too much of a stretch to say the "great cloud of witnesses" surrounding us (Hebrews 12:1) does the same?

When we pray for our children to grow in their faith, we're praying for the very thing God longs for them to do. And He gives us this assurance in His Word: "This is the confidence we have in approaching God: that if we ask anything according to his will, he hears us" (1 John 5:14).

God is listening. Ask away.

Day 8

GROWING UP IN YOU

Like newborn babies, crave pure spiritual
milk, so that by it you may grow up in your
salvation, now that you have tasted that
the Lord is good.

1 Peter 2:2–3

No matter how much they grow, they are always our 'babies.'

The miracle of life is such a breathtaking gift from your
hand and your heart, Lord!

I could never forget the moment I became a parent. I praise
you for the wonder and gift of a child. How blessed I am!

You've given me this dear one for a reason, and your Word
makes that clear.

Throughout life we are to point them to you, to "bring them
up in the training and instruction of the Lord" (Ephesians 6:4).

Growing in a relationship with you is the most important
thing of all!

Everything else pales in comparison: achievements, degrees,
careers . . . "For what will it profit a man if he gains the
whole world and forfeits his soul?" (Matthew 16:26[a]).

So I'm going to love with my prayers this one you have given me.

I thank you that because you have had mercy on me and I am "counted as righteous" in you (Romans 4:5[b]) so that even my prayers are "powerful and effective" (James 5:16).

More than anything else, I pray my child "may grow up in" the salvation that you so freely give (1 Peter 2:2).

I pray that he will "believe" that you are "the Messiah, the Son of God, and that by believing" in you, he "will have life by the power of" your name (John 20:31[c]).

I pray he will "taste and see" that you are "good," and know "the joys of those who take refuge" in you (Psalm 34:8[d]).

I want my child to know your love most of all, because there is nothing better! "Your love is better than life" (Psalm 63:3)!

I also want him to know your Word, because he does not "live by bread alone, but by every word" that comes from your mouth (Matthew 4:4[e]).

This incredible gift of salvation you have given me is the inheritance I want to share with this one I love, "an inheritance that can never perish, spoil or fade . . . kept in heaven" (1 Peter 1:4).

Father, I pray he will want you more than anything else, and that "your name and renown" will be "the desire" of his heart forever (Isaiah 26:8).

I pray he will love you with all his "heart," "soul," "strength" and "mind" (Luke 10:27[f]).

"How great is the goodness you have stored up" for those who love you and "fear you" (Psalm 31:19[g])!

If he trusts in you, he "will lack no good thing!" (Psalm 34:10[h]).

a ESV, b NLT, c NLT, d NLT, e ESV, f NKJV, g NLT, h NLT

Day 9

ROOTS AND WINGS

"But blessed are those who trust in the
    Lord and have made the Lord
their hope and confidence. They are like
    trees planted along a riverbank,
with roots that reach deep into the water.
    Such trees are not bothered by the
    heat or worried by long months of
    drought. Their leaves stay green,
and they never stop producing fruit."
Jeremiah 17:7–8 (NLT)

I've heard it said that a child needs 'roots' and 'wings,' Lord. Roots to understand where he comes from, and wings to lift him where he needs to go.

Today I ask for both.

I pray you will give him 'roots' to humbly understand that he comes from you. You are "the everlasting God, the Creator of the ends of the earth" (Isaiah 40:28ᵃ).

Help him to understand that his body is much more than just a mass of cells cobbled together by cosmic coincidence. You "made us, and we are" yours (Psalm 100:3)!

"Long ago you laid the foundation of the earth and made the heavens with your hands" (Psalm 102:25[b]).

May he praise you for his life and all the gifts you've given him—and never take your kindness for granted!

When the world tells him to have confidence in himself, I pray he will make *you* his "hope and confidence" instead (Jeremiah 17:7[c]). Then he will grow strong in you, "like trees planted along a riverbank," that keep "producing fruit" (Jeremiah 17:7–8[d]).

Lord Jesus, I pray he will be "rooted and established in love" because you have made yourself at home in his heart "through faith" (Ephesians 3:17).

Then his roots will hold through every storm, because you are "good, a strong refuge when trouble comes." You are "close to those who trust" in you (Nahum 1:7[e]).

With roots like that, he will have wings as well!

You promise in your Word that "those who trust in" you "will find new strength. They will soar high on wings like eagles" (Isaiah 40:31[f]).

I want to see him soar, Lord, lifted to new heights of your love!

"Your unfailing love is as high as the heavens. Your faithfulness reaches to the clouds" (Psalm 57:10[g]). "The heavens, even the highest heaven, cannot contain you" (1 Kings 8:27)!

"No eye has seen, no ear has heard, and no mind has imagined" what you have "prepared for those who love" you (1 Corinthians 2:9[h]).

I pray he will love you, Lord! May he love you "with all" his heart, soul, mind and strength (Mark 12:30)!

Then he will be blessed beyond my power to ask, and discover for himself that there is never a limit to the love that you give!

a ESV, b NLT, c NLT, d NLT, e NLT, f NLT, g NLT, h NLT

CARRIED HOME

"I have cared for you since you were born.
   Yes, I carried you
before you were born. I will be your God
   throughout your lifetime—
until your hair is white with age. I made
   you, and I will care for you.
I will carry you along and save you."

Isaiah 46:3–4 (NLT)

"I will carry you along and save you" (Isaiah 46:4[a]).

Yes, Lord! That's what I want for my child.

You have saved me and carried me through life, and I'm grateful.

I know what David meant when he wrote, "Praise the Lord; praise God our Savior! For each day he carries us in his arms. Our God is a God who saves!" (Psalm 68:19–20[b]).

I remember when I could carry my child in my arms and I treasured those moments. There have been so many times since that I wish I could do what I did then—pick her up and hold her and keep her from harm.

But there's a limit to what I can do for my child. My arms are only so strong—unlike yours! Yours are the "everlasting arms" (Deuteronomy 33:27[c])!

You "will not grow tired or weary" (Isaiah 40:28). There's no limit to what you can do!

When she was little and she'd fall asleep I could scoop her up and place her safely in her bed. My heart toward her hasn't changed—I love her and want to keep her from harm. So I ask that you do what I cannot.

I pray you will wrap your arms around her and "surround" her "with your favor" (Psalm 5:12).

Because you made her, I ask that you "care for" her until her "hair is white with age" (Isaiah 46:4[d]). Please take care of her in those days when I won't be there to help!

I pray that she will "draw near" to you "with a sincere heart and with the full assurance that faith brings" (Hebrews 10:22), so that she will know the "comfort and salvation" (2 Corinthians 1:6[e]) that only come from you.

May she trust in you "at all times," and "pour out" her heart to you (Psalm 62:8[f]), so that she may be enthralled with "the joy of your presence" (Psalm 21:6) and caught up in the wonder of all that you are.

You told your people once, "your little daughters will be carried home" (Isaiah 60:4[g]). I want that for her as well, Lord, in this way: I ask that you carry her *all the way* home. I pray she will not only wake up in the beauty of your presence each day. . . .

I ask that when her work on this earth is done, your strong arms will bear her to heaven, and she will awaken anew to the morning of eternity with you.

a NLT, b NLT, c ESV, d NLT, e ESV, f NLT, g NLT

Day 11

"PICK ME!"

Then I heard the Lord asking,
"Whom should I send as a messenger
to this people? Who will go for us?"
I said, "Here I am. Send me."

Isaiah 6:8 (NLT)

Sometimes choosing teams can be rough, Lord.

No matter our age, whether we're playing kickball or meeting in the board room, no one likes being the last one picked.

You understand this better than anyone, Jesus! You, "the image of the invisible God, the firstborn over all creation" (Colossians 1:15ᵃ), were "despised and rejected by mankind, a man of suffering, and familiar with pain," like "one from whom people hide their faces" (Isaiah 53:3).

You know better than anyone else how we size each other up and misjudge each other with just a look!

But *you* don't do that, and I'm so grateful. You told us, "Whoever comes to me I will never drive away" (John 6:37).

I praise you for your open arms, Lord. How you long for us to come to you!

You wait so patiently for us. Your "patience gives people time to be saved" (2 Peter 3:15[b]).

And you not only save us, you give us an incomparable gift. You give us your Holy Spirit "as a guarantee" of the unlimited life we will enjoy with you (2 Corinthians 5:5[c]). You've "poured out" your "love into our hearts" (Romans 5:5)!

Your Spirit gives us gifts as well, "gifts" to encourage and strengthen others and "build up the church" (1 Corinthians 14:12).

You never stop giving, Lord!

I pray that my son will use "whatever gift" he has received "to serve others" (1 Peter 4:10) in a way that will bless them and please you.

Help him to understand that you want us to share what you give, and as we do we are blessed all the more.

I ask that he will be "eager to serve" you (1 Peter 5:2), and that he will serve others for you "with much enthusiasm and on his own initiative" (2 Corinthians 8:17).

When you want to send someone to share your truth and you ask, "Who will go for us?", may he respond, "Here I am. Send me" (Isaiah 6:8[d]).

I pray that the good news will resound from his life "with power, with the Holy Spirit and deep conviction" (1 Thessalonians 1:5).

I pray he will "show genuine concern" in others' well-being (Philippians 2:20) because your love is working through him.

Thank you for the purpose you give us in life, Lord Jesus! You were "rejected by humans but chosen by God and precious to him" (1 Peter 2:4), so that we may be chosen too!

I pray my son will embrace this truth with all of his heart, so that he "may declare the praises" of you who called him "out of darkness into" your "wonderful light" (1 Peter 2:9).

a NKJV, b NLT, c ESV, d NLT

"MORE!"

May God give you more and more mercy,
peace, and love.

Jude 2 (NLT)

More!

It doesn't take us too long to learn that word, does it, Father?

We want so much! But so much of what we want is not good for us, and only you can help us sort that out.

I think of some times I have asked you for something and you mercifully did not answer in the way I wanted . . . It was difficult then, but I'm grateful now!

So today I ask for the most important gift my child could ever have, and I believe it's a prayer you would love to answer . . . I simply ask for more of you in my child's life.

I will leave to your perfect wisdom what she needs most, but I pray for "more and more" of your "mercy, peace and love" (Jude 2[a]) to flow into her soul.

Lord Jesus, just as you "grew in wisdom and stature, and in favor with God" and others (Luke 2:52), I pray my daughter will grow in every way in you.

What could she possibly need more than you?

"Godliness with contentment is great gain" (1 Timothy 6:6), and I pray she will be profoundly content in you.

Paul "learned the secret of being content in any and every situation" (Philippians 4:12) because he found his strength in you.

Please give her grace to understand that you are the best thing in her life.

"Cast but a glance at riches, and they are gone"—they "sprout wings and fly off to the sky like an eagle" (Proverbs 23:5).

But under your "wings" she "will find refuge" and rest secure (Psalm 91:4).

"You are good and do only good" (Psalm 119:68[b]). There is no one and nothing better than you!

May she say, "LORD, you alone are my inheritance, my cup of blessing" (Psalm 16:5[c]).

May she drink deeply from you, so that the "living water" you give her "becomes a fresh, bubbling spring within," giving her "eternal life" (John 4:11, 14[d]).

"You have performed many wonders for us. Your plans for us are too numerous to list. You have no equal. If I tried to recite all your wonderful deeds, I would never come to the end of them" (Psalm 40:5[e]).

No matter what may happen in her life, may she always "keep on hoping for your help" and "praise you more and more" (Psalm 71:14[f]).

"May your glorious name be praised! May it be exalted above all blessing and praise!" (Nehemiah 9:5[g]).

You "must increase," but we "must decrease" (John 3:30[h]).
I pray for more and more of you in her life!

a NLT, b NLT, c NLT, d NLT, e NLT, f NLT, g NLT, h NASB

GIVE TO LOVE, LOVE TO GIVE

"Give, and it will be given to you. A good measure, pressed down, shaken together and running over, will be poured into your lap. For with the measure you use, it will be measured to you."

Luke 6:38

Father, why is it that the smallest children give so freely?

Little ones open their hands and give what's in them. They seem to value the act of sharing and giving more than they value the things in their grasp.

But that doesn't last long. The more we grow, the more our hands close until they are balled in tiny fists and our little mouths are screaming, 'Me! Me! Me! Mine! Mine! Mine!'

Unless you give us grace, we never grow out of that attitude. We just become more subtle in our selfishness and more skillful in covering it up.

So today I pray that my child will "excel in this grace of giving" (2 Corinthians 8:7). I pray he will be like you and love to give.

It gave you "great pleasure" to give yourself to us and "adopt us into" your "own family" (Ephesians 1:5ᵃ). You are "so rich in kindness and grace" that you "purchased our freedom with the blood" of your Son "and forgave our sins" (Ephesians 1:7ᵇ).

You have "showered" your "kindness on us" (Ephesians 1:8ᶜ) and blessed us with your Spirit, "so we can know the wonderful things" you have "freely given us" (1 Corinthians 2:12ᵈ).

You keep giving to us every day. "You open your hand and satisfy the desires of every living thing" (Psalm 145:16).

Your Word says that you love "a person who gives cheerfully" (2 Corinthians 9:7ᵉ); I pray he will discover the joy of giving so you will love the way he gives!

May he love to give because he loves you, and give out of a sense of gratitude for all you have given him. I pray that his "love will overflow more and more," and that he "will keep on growing in knowledge and understanding" of how blessed he is in you (Philippians 1:9ᶠ).

Lord Jesus, you promised that if he gives he will receive. "It will be given" to him in "good measure, pressed down, shaken together and running over" (Luke 6:38).

I pray he will love to give to those in need, because your Word teaches that "whoever is kind to the poor lends to the Lord," and you "will reward" him for what he has done (Proverbs 19:17). You even tell us that "whoever gives to the poor will lack nothing" (Proverbs 28:27ᵍ)!

"Good will come to those who are generous and lend freely" (Psalm 112:5). May he give "generously'" so that he "will also reap generously" (2 Corinthians 9:6)!

"With the measure" he uses, "it will be measured" to him (Luke 6:38); so may his hands and heart be open and his measure great.

And may he love to give to *you* most of all! When he gives to those in need may he see you in their faces, and love serving you in them, until the day he hears you say "whatever you did for one of the least of these . . . you did for me" (Matthew 25:40).

BACK TO SCHOOL

Get wisdom, get understanding; do not
forget my words
or turn from them. Do not forsake wisdom,
and she will protect you;
love her, and she will watch over you.
The beginning of wisdom is this: Get
wisdom.
Though it cost all you have, get
understanding.

Proverbs 4:5–7

I pray my child will never stop learning, Lord.

There is so much to learn, and the more we learn the more we understand how much we don't know!

But you know everything. You are "a wonderful teacher" (Isaiah 28:29ª), "whose wisdom is magnificent" (Isaiah 28:29).

Wisdom comes from you! And I ask that you give it to her. You are the One who "gives wisdom to the wise and knowledge to the discerning" (Daniel 2:21).

True learning starts with you. Your Word teaches us that "The fear of the LORD is the beginning of wisdom, and the knowledge of the Holy One is understanding" (Proverbs 9:10).

So I ask that she learn to pray, "Teach me to do your will, for you are my God. May your gracious Spirit lead me forward on a firm footing" (Psalm 143:10[b]).

From your "mouth come knowledge and understanding" (Proverbs 2:6). I pray that she will "listen to" your "instructions," and "store them" in her "heart" (Job 22:22[c]).

Most of all, Lord Jesus, I ask that she will "grow in the grace and knowledge" of you as her "Lord and Savior," so that she may live for your "glory both now and forever!" (2 Peter 3:18).

Help her to understand that there is more to learning than the mere accumulation of information. No matter how much she learns and grows, I pray she will always "crave" the "pure spiritual milk" of your truth so that she "will grow into a full experience of salvation" (1 Peter 2:2[d]).

Watch over her learning, Lord. Guide her in it and guard her heart so that it is pleasing to you.

There are so many lessons to learn in life! I pray she will sit at your feet and learn the ones of your choosing.

"You delight in truth in the inward being," and "you teach" us "wisdom in the secret heart" (Psalm 51:6[e]).

I pray she "may gain a heart of wisdom" (Psalm 90:12), by understanding that life on earth is brief and eternity is long.

I pray she will learn to value your wisdom over human wisdom. "Many are the plans in the mind of a man," but it is your "purpose" that "will stand" (Proverbs 19:21[f]).

Your "wisdom is sweet" to the "soul." If she finds it, she
   "will have a bright future" (Proverbs 24:14[g])!
So I pray that she will! "Wisdom lights up a person's face"
   (Ecclesiastes 8:1[h]). May hers shine with your light and
   love and wisdom forever!

a NLT, b NLT, c NLT, d NLT, e ESV, f ESV, g NLT, h NLT

Week 3

WALKING

Reach Beyond Touch

While I was yet walking in sin, often
attempting to rise, and sinking still deeper,
my dear mother, in vigorous hope,
persisted in earnest prayer for me.

Augustine

Some years back my sister and her family took a long walk. They started on the beach at their home in Ventura, California, and nine months and thirty-one hundred miles later arrived in Yorktown, Virginia. They had walked from one end of the continental United States to the other.

"Why are you doing this?" I asked my sister before she left.

"Because time passes quickly and our children are only young once. We want to slow life down to a walk."

I didn't get it at the time—I only saw the challenges and dangers. But my sister saw the chance to just *be* with her kids for a while as the world rushed by.

Once I had children of my own, I began to understand. There are those moments you don't want to let go of. The soft, round cheek pressed against your own. The gentle breathing of a tiny loved one safe and warm in your hands. The little hands holding tightly to your own as she takes her first steps. . . . If there were only a way to rewind life and relive those moments, you'd do it again and again.

Children grow and gradually letting them go isn't easy. Because we love them we wish we could always keep them from harm and help when there's a need. But as they grow they will go to places where we cannot follow, and in time they must choose their own roads.

Still, there is a way we can be there for them. Where our hands cannot reach, our hearts and prayers can. It was Robert Browning who wrote, "Ah, but a man's reach should exceed his grasp, or what's a heaven for?"[2] Because our Father in heaven is faithful to answer prayer, through Him we can offer help far beyond any natural ability we have. And because He remembers our prayers perfectly, we can even touch our children's lives far beyond our years.

When our children first learn to walk, we hold their hands to steady them and hold them up. We cannot walk with them through life, but our prayers can steady them. You might imagine placing your child's hand in the hand of Jesus. Children must decide whether they will walk with Him in the moment, but our prayers can even help them with that decision.

This week we'll pray that our children will choose to walk with God wherever they go. These are prayers built on the promises of the Twenty-Third Psalm that point to the "good shepherd," Jesus (John 10:11). He is the One who restores our souls and brings us safely "through the valley of

2. Browning, Robert. *Men and Women,* "Andrea del Sarto," lines 97–98.

the shadow of death" (Psalm 23:4 ESV). He meets us in our place of deepest need and leads us in "paths of righteousness" (Psalm 23:2 ESV) all the way home. Without Him, we wander in hard places and are lost. With Him, green pastures and still waters await.

We cannot follow our children "all the days" of their lives, but "goodness and mercy" will (Psalm 23:6 ESV) if the Shepherd leads them.

These are prayers to slow life down to a walk. The one walk that really matters.

ALL HE NEEDS

The LORD is my shepherd, I lack nothing.

Psalm 23:1

Sometimes my mind is filled with thoughts of all that my child needs, Father. But he has no greater need than you.

David understood that you are our deepest need, and because he did he was "a man after" your "own heart" (1 Samuel 13:14[a]).

I pray my son will "long for you" (Psalm 42:1[b]) with a yearning deeper than emotion.

Just as he sometimes held on to me so tightly when he was little, I ask that his soul will "cling to you," and that he may know your "strong right hand holds" him "securely" (Psalm 63:8[c]).

When he gets up in the morning, let him "hunger and thirst for righteousness." Only then will he really "be satisfied" (Matthew 5:6[d])!

Just as David wrote, "When I awake, I will be satisfied with seeing" you (Psalm 17:15), I pray he will feel the need to spend time with you in your Word, opening his heart to you every day. Please give him "a tender, responsive heart" to your Spirit (Ezekiel 11:19e)!

I pray that "the eyes" of his "heart" will be filled with your light, so that he "may know the hope" you alone can give (Ephesians 1:18).

When the world tells him he has to have something, turn his "eyes from looking at worthless things" (Psalm 119:37f) and let him find his heart's desire in you.

"A craving for everything we see, and pride in our achievements and possessions" are not from you (1 John 2:16g).

Keep him from the worries, debts, and burdens that craving the things of this world can cause. Give him wisdom to understand that "the borrower is slave to the lender" (Proverbs 22:7), and "one's life does not consist in the abundance of the things he possesses" (Luke 12:15h).

You have come that he might "have life and have it abundantly" (John 10:10i)!

I pray you will be his source of life in all things, Lord Jesus!

I pray he will not need *things* to make him happy, but will instead learn "the secret of being content in any and every situation, whether well fed or hungry, whether living in plenty or in want" (Philippians 4:12). Let him understand that he really can "do everything through" you who give him "strength" (Philippians 4:13j)!

"This world is fading away, along with everything that people crave. But anyone who does what pleases" you "will live forever" (1 John 2:17k).

Thank you that we can please you, Father. Because you are so "rich in mercy" (Ephesians 2:4), even we "who once

were far away have been brought near" because of Jesus'
kindness to us through the cross (Ephesians 2:13).

I pray that my son's soul "will be fully satisfied as with the
richest of foods" (Psalm 63:5). May He always be satisfied in you!

a ESV, b NLT, c NLT, d ESV, e NLT, f NKJV, g NLT, h NKJV, i ESV, j NLT, k NLT

THE GOOD SHEPHERD

He makes me lie down in green pastures,
he leads me beside quiet waters.

Psalm 23:2

You really are "the good shepherd," Lord Jesus.

You did exactly what you said you would. You gave your own "life for the sheep" (John 10:11ᵃ).

Because you died on the cross to save us from our sins, if we "receive" you and have faith in you (John 1:12), "we have peace with God through" you (Romans 5:1). You are "our peace" (Ephesians 2:14)!

Good Shepherd, I pray my child will "find rest" for her soul in you (Matthew 11:29).

You are "the God of all comfort" (2 Corinthians 1:3) who calms our restless hearts with your "perfect love" that "drives out fear" (1 John 4:18).

You even give "songs in the night" (Job 35:10)—a reason to praise you when all others fail. You are that reason! You are always "deserving of praise" (Psalm 48:1ᵇ)!

Because you "have overcome the world," even though we face "many trials and sorrows" we may "have peace" in you (John 16:33[c]).

How my precious daughter needs you, Lord Jesus. How I need you!

Thank you that regardless of the circumstances we face in life, because "your name is near" (Psalm 75:1[d]), your peace is always accessible.

I pray my daughter will always know your peace deeply in her heart because she will always "revere" you "as Lord" (1 Peter 3:15).

I pray she will "listen to" your voice (John 10:16[e]) and follow you through every path you have planned to lead her safely home.

May she daily "ask where the good way is," and walk with you so closely that she always finds "rest" for her soul (Jeremiah 6:16).

May your green pastures, "the richest of fare" (Isaiah 55:2), satisfy her every need.

May she know the quiet waters of your "wells of salvation" and drink "deeply" from them "with joy" (Isaiah 12:3[f, g]).

Wonderful Shepherd! How kind you are! Even when we have wandered you "go after the lost sheep" until you find it (Luke 15:4).

I praise you because you have promised, "I will seek the lost, and I will bring back the strayed, and I will bind up the injured, and I will strengthen the weak" (Ezekiel 34:16[h])!

May my daughter be "your special possession" whom you lead "like a shepherd," and carry "in your arms forever" (Psalm 28:9ⁱ)!

a NKJV, b NLT, c NLT, d ESV, e NLT, f NKJV, g NLT, h ESV, i NLT

RESTORED

> He restores my soul; He leads me in
> the paths of righteousness for His name's
> sake.
>
> Psalm 23:3 (NKJV)

You do such beautiful things, Father!

"I am filled with awe by your amazing works" (Habakkuk 3:2[a]).

I think of when my child was born. . . . Two little hands, two tiny feet . . .

What a miracle you've placed in my life, Lord!

I praise you for the gift of a child—"How amazing" are the things you do! Everything you do reveals your "glory and majesty!" (Psalm 111:2–3[b]).

You even restore our souls. I think of what you've saved me from and how your Word describes all you have done for me. It tells me, "you were cleansed; you were made holy; you were made right with God by calling on the name of the Lord Jesus Christ and by the Spirit of our God" (1 Corinthians 6:11[c]).

I praise you that because of your incredible mercy I am not what I once was.

You said, "I have seen his ways, and will heal him; I will also lead him, and restore comforts to him" (Isaiah 57:18ᵈ).

I was once "dead" in my many sins, but you made me "alive with Christ" (Ephesians 2:5)! You saved me "from the empty life" I was living and ransomed me with "the precious blood of Christ, the sinless, spotless Lamb" (1 Peter 1:18–19ᵉ).

Once you save us, you're just getting started. You strengthen us and protect what you began, helping us grow "in every way more and more like Christ" (Ephesians 4:15ᶠ).

How amazing it is that you help us change so that we are able to leave old sins behind. When the devil attacks us and we "resist him," you "restore, confirm, strengthen, and establish" us (1 Peter 5:9–10ᵍ).

I pray that my son will always rely on your saving grace and strength, Father. You are "the LORD who heals" (Exodus 15:26ʰ)!

Just as you sent your healing power ahead of another who came to you years ago—when you told him in that moment, "Let it be done just as you believed it would" (Matthew 8:13)—I ask that you send your restoring, healing touch ahead into the moments when my son needs it most. And I believe that you will!

I believe you will restore him because you are faithful to "lead" us "along the right path" (Psalm 27:11ⁱ), according to your wisdom which never fails.

I believe you will restore him because it will bring "honor" to your "name" (Psalm 23:3ʲ).

I believe you will restore him because you have promised that you "who began the good work" in us will continue "until it is finally finished on the day when Christ Jesus returns" (Philippians 1:6[k])!

a NLT, b NLT, c NLT, d NKJV, e NLT, f NLT, g ESV, h NKJV, i NLT, j NLT, k NLT

STRENGTH IN THE VALLEY

Even though I walk through the valley
of the shadow of death,
I will fear no evil, for you are with me;
your rod and your staff, they comfort me.

Psalm 23:4 ESV

All of us have to walk our own valleys.

Your Word says that every "heart knows its own bitterness, and no one else can share its joy" (Proverbs 14:10).

There are places my child will go where I cannot follow, and heartaches he will know that I cannot share or spare him from—even though I long to, just because I love him.

But as I bring him before you today, I'm reminded that you love him even more, and can help and bless him through my prayers.

With you, "all things are possible" (Matthew 19:26[a])!

So I ask that you will always meet my child in the valley, Lord.

You can go where I never could, and be with him in moments and years far beyond my reach.

Even when he walks "through the valley of the shadow of death," when "you are with" him, he need "fear no evil" (Psalm 23:4[b]).

With you, "every valley shall be lifted up" (Isaiah 40:4[c])!

You can give him comfort and strength in the darkest and most difficult situation. You can even turn his "darkness into light" (Psalm 18:28)!

Your "light shines in the darkness, and the darkness can never extinguish it" (John 1:5[d]).

David knew this from the personal experience of your presence and protection. That's why he wrote, "The LORD is my light and my salvation—so why should I be afraid? The LORD is my fortress, protecting me from danger, so why should I tremble?" (Psalm 27:1[e]).

Day or night, you "neither slumber nor sleep" (Psalm 121:4[f]). You are always watching "over all who love" and follow you (Psalm 145:20).

So I pray he will. I pray he will always run to you as his fortress and live "in Your light" (Psalm 36:9[g]).

Help him to "carefully determine what pleases" you (Ephesians 5:10[h]), and "have nothing to do with the fruitless deeds of darkness" (Ephesians 5:11).

Then, no matter what darkness may fall, he will be ready for it. "Even in darkness light dawns for the upright, for those who are gracious and compassionate and righteous" (Psalm 112:4).

If he takes shelter in you, "the Most High," "no evil will conquer" him (Psalm 91:9–10[i]).

May the rod of your protection and conviction keep him "from the devil's trap" (2 Timothy 2:26ʲ) and the staff of your "tender mercy" guide him firmly in "the path of peace" (Luke 1:78–79).

A PLACE AT YOUR TABLE

You prepare a table before me in the
presence of my enemies.
You anoint my head with oil; my cup
overflows.

Psalm 23:5

When David wrote that you prepared "a table" for him "in the presence" of his enemies, wasn't it because you had given him strength in the face of adversity?

I ask that for my child as well.

I pray that no matter what obstacles she faces, she will be able to say, "I thank Christ Jesus our Lord, who has given me strength to do his work" (1 Timothy 1:12ᵃ).

My prayer is not that you would be on her side, but that she would be on yours. Then she will always win, even when she seems to lose (in the world's eyes), because your "weakness is stronger than the greatest of human strength" (1 Corinthians 1:25ᵇ). Your "power is made perfect in weakness" (2 Corinthians 12:9ᶜ)!

"There is no wisdom, no insight, no plan that can succeed against" you (Proverbs 21:30).

All of history is heading in your direction. "The wicked plot against the godly; they snarl at them in defiance." But you see the "day of judgment coming" (Psalm 37:12–13[d]).

It is the table on that day that matters most of all.

Lord Jesus, you promised that "people will come from east and west, and from north and south," and sit at the "table in the kingdom of God" (Luke 13:29[e]). I pray that I will sit beside her there in your presence!

But we have a journey to finish before we can get there, unless you return today. Until the day you come back, I pray you will fill her with your Holy Spirit and anoint her with your "oil of joy" (Psalm 45:7).

Even in the middle of the world's adversity, I ask that she "feast on the abundance of your house" and "drink from your river of delights" (Psalm 36:8) as she worships you and discovers the soul-satisfaction only you can give.

May she "lift up the cup of salvation" and "praise" your name for "saving" her (Psalm 116:13[f])!

I pray that she will know you to be her "strength every morning," and her "salvation in time of distress" (Isaiah 33:2).

I pray she will look for the good you alone can bring regardless of what the world throws at her.

May her own prayer be, "O my Strength," you are "the God who shows me unfailing love" (Psalm 59:17[g]). "O my strength, I will watch for you" (Psalm 59:9[h])!

Help us both always to look forward to you, and "be always on the watch, and pray" (Luke 21:36)!

"Come, Lord Jesus" (Revelation 22:20)!

a NLT, b NLT, c ESV, d NLT, e ESV, f NLT, g NLT, h ESV

RESCUED BY LOVE

Surely your goodness and unfailing love
will pursue me all the days of my life.

PSALM 23:6 (NLT)

I'm so glad you pursued me, Lord.

You went after me to bring me home; you came "to seek and to save the lost" (Luke 19:10[a]).

No matter how much it cost you, you never gave up on me. "How priceless your faithful love is!" (Psalm 36:7[b]).

Your love hasn't just looked for me—it's found me. I can't imagine living without "your great mercy and love" (Psalm 25:6).

"You are God my Savior, and my hope is in you all day long" (Psalm 25:5)!

I want this for my daughter too, Lord. I pray she will always "take hold of the hope offered to us" and so be "greatly encouraged" (Hebrews 6:18).

When I think about how much I love her, I'm humbled by the truth that you love her even more. She is your creation! "You knit" her "together" (Psalm 139:13), and you "long for the work of your hands" (Job 14:15[c]).

Just as you came after me, you went for her as well. I praise you that you have pursued her with the very same passion and love.

Thank you for your amazing search and rescue mission, Father. You could have snapped your fingers and called an end to everything because of the way we have all "rebelled against you" (Nehemiah 9:26[d]).

Yet you did not send your "Son into the world to condemn the world, but to save the world through him" (John 3:17)!

I pray she will always treasure this truth: that you loved her so much that you would die to save her, Lord Jesus.

Help her to "press on to take hold of that" for which you "took hold" of her (Philippians 3:12), so that she may "take hold of the life that is truly life" (1 Timothy 6:19).

I pray she will "have the power to understand," as all your people should, "how wide, how long, how high, and how deep" your love is (Ephesians 3:18[e]).

May she truly, deeply experience your love, Lord Jesus, "though it is too great to understand fully." Then she "will be made complete with all the fullness of life and power" that comes from you (Ephesians 3:19[f]).

"Surround" her "with your tender mercies," so that she "may live" and love you now and forever! (Psalm 119:77[g]).

Thank you that your "goodness and love will follow" her "all the days" of her life (Psalm 23:6), to draw her ever nearer to you, and to bring her safely home.

a ESV, b NIrV, c ESV, d ESV, e NLT, f NLT, g NLT

BARE FEET ON GOLDEN STREETS

And I will dwell in the house of the Lord forever.

Psalm 23:6

I ask that my child will be with you forever, Lord. Even as I pray, I can see him there "by faith" (Hebrews 11:13), ever joyful in your presence. And I long to be there with him one day and watch him "gaze upon" your "beauty" (Psalm 27:4[a]) and worship you "in the splendor" of your holiness (1 Chronicles 16:29).

Father, I praise you that there "are many rooms" in your "house" (John 14:2[b]). I pray he "will dwell" in one of them (Psalm 23:6)!

How good it will be to be free once and for all from sin and self—the "old sinful nature" (Ephesians 4:22[c])—and run barefoot on your streets of "pure gold" (Revelation 21:21[d])!

I want to do whatever I can to help him get there, Father, so I kneel before you today as "your servant" (Psalm 116:16[e]).

As I pray for him today, I acknowledge that high above my thoughts of diplomas, careers, or even grandchildren, and far beyond any hope or dream or plan I may have for him, your purpose matters most of all. You've blessed me with him so I may bless him with you!

The single most valuable, lasting thing I could ever do as a parent is point my child to you, so that he may "know you, the only true God, and Jesus Christ, whom you have sent" (John 17:3).

I ask that you will help me to do my best to live before him as a "good example" (1 Peter 5:3[f]) so that he will be drawn to you through me.

Please give me the grace I need "not to put any stumbling block or obstacle" in his way (Romans 14:13), and the wisdom to show him the "straight paths" (Proverbs 4:11[g]) that lead to you!

Lord Jesus, you said that, "If anyone loves me, he will keep my word, and my Father will love him, and we will come to him and make our home with him" (John 14:23[h]). I praise you for that promise!

I ask that he will learn to love you and obey you so he will experience the incomparable joy of having his heart 'at home' with you in this world and the next.

May he love simply to be with you, spending time with you in prayer and in your Word.

I pray he will "rejoice in your word like one who discovers a great treasure" (Psalm 119:162[i])!

Beautiful Savior, please give him grace to walk with you "in the light," so that he may enjoy a close and tender relationship with the Father because of your perfect sacrifice for us on the cross that "purifies us from all sin" (1 John 1:7).

May your light lead him all the way home, Lord! Then, in the city that "does not need the sun or the moon to shine on it" because "the glory of God gives it light, and the Lamb is its lamp" (Revelation 21:23), we will praise you forever and ever!

a ESV, b ESV, c NLT, d ESV, e NLT, f NLT, g NLT, h ESV, i NLT

Week 4

LOVING

Love and an Ugly Mug

Love is patient, love is kind. It does not
    envy, it does not boast, it is not proud.
It does not dishonor others, it is not
    self-seeking,
it is not easily angered, it keeps no record
    of wrongs.
Love does not delight in evil but rejoices
    with the truth.
It always protects, always trusts, always
    hopes, always perseveres.
Love never fails.

1 Corinthians 13:4–8

To the untrained eye it was nothing more than an ugly mug. The paint had worn off long before, and the only visible marking was a tiny, gray hairline crack working its way down from the rim.

But the mug stayed in use. For nearly three decades until the day he died, my dad would drink his morning coffee from it. Day after day, year after year, that mug carried a message. It simply said, "I love you."

I gave Dad the mug when I was twelve years old. We had stopped for dinner at a popular chain restaurant which had several of the mugs in a display case. I overheard Dad say that he liked them, so I used the last of my allowance to buy one.

Only time would tell how much that meant to him. When you're a parent you hang on to some things because of the worth your kids bring to them. The clay trivet from second grade decorated with smiley faces. That middle school water color where the paint runs together. The old worn and stained stuffed animal . . . They all have a way of sticking around simply because of the love that went into them.

Love at its best shows up in the smallest and most practical ways—ways that sometimes don't make sense to a self-focused world. That's why "love is patient, love is kind. . . . It does not dishonor others, it is not self-seeking, it is not easily angered, it keeps no record of wrongs" (1 Corinthians 13:4–5). This kind of love isn't easy, but it *is* possible—because "God's love has been poured out into our hearts through the Holy Spirit, who has been given to us" (Romans 5:5).

In the next several pages we'll pray our way through all the characteristics of love described in 1 Corinthians 13, with the hope that our children's lives may be filled to overflowing with God's love. Then lasting love may spill over from them into others who see our "down to earth" Savior in them.

Genuine love is so much more than something we feel. It's something we *do*. These are prayers that our children may "follow the way of love" (1 Corinthians 14:1), and so follow God.

LEGACY OF LOVE

And yet I will show you the most excellent
way. . . . Love is patient, love is kind.

1 Corinthians 12:31, 13:4

Please help my child to understand what real love is, Father.

"Love comes from" you (1 John 4:7[a]). It was your idea to begin with!

You are the source of real love; love that is genuine, lasting, and true. "This is real love—not that we loved" you, but that you "loved us" and sent your Son "as a sacrifice to take away our sins" (1 John 4:10[b]).

You are "love"! We can "know and rely on the love" you have for us (1 John 4:16). Your love is entirely trustworthy, "the best way of all" (1 Corinthians 12:31[c])!

When we let you love through us, we find ourselves able to love in a way that would never be possible in our own strength.

You transform our hearts with your love! The closer we walk with you, the more you help us to love the things you love and "keep in step with the Spirit" (Galatians 5:25).

I pray that my daughter will always "walk in love" and obedience with you (2 John 6). Please fill her with your Spirit so her heart overflows with your love, Lord Jesus!

Only you can show us how to make love work, and I pray that my daughter will understand this.

Our world is filled with so many counterfeit notions of what love is. We define it on our own terms and then wonder why it shatters in our hands and lies broken at our feet.

Please give her the wisdom to see that true love is more than something we 'fall' into.

I pray that you will help her to comprehend that real love is more than simply a feeling or emotion—it is something we *choose* when we are obedient to you.

That is why you went to the cross and "suffered for" us, leaving us "an example" in love (1 Peter 2:21), and why your Word tells us, "let us not love with words or speech but with actions and in truth" (1 John 3:18).

The love you give is "patient and kind" (1 Corinthians 13:4[d]); you help us to love when it is not easy and doesn't come naturally to us.

I pray that you will be the love of her life, and that you will lead her in love! Love begins with you. "We love" you because you "first loved us" (1 John 4:19[e]), and you "pour out your unfailing love on those who love you" (Psalm 36:10[f]).

I ask you to help me set an example for my child as well, so that she will see you in me. "No one has ever seen" you. "But if we love each other, you live in us, and your "love is brought to full expression in us" (1 John 4:12[g]).

I want to leave your legacy of love in my child's life, Lord.

Your Word promises that your "love is with those who fear" you and your "righteousness" is "with their children's children" (Psalm 103:17)!

I praise you because your "love endures forever," and your "faithfulness continues through all generations" (Psalm 100:5)!

a NLT, b NLT, c NIrV, d NLT, e NKJV, f NLT, g NLT

BRAGGING RIGHT

Love . . . does not envy or boast; it is not
arrogant. . . .
"Let the one who boasts, boast in the
Lord."

1 Corinthians 13:4,
2 Corinthians 10:17 (ESV)

I pray that my child's heart will be so filled with your love that there will be no room in his life for pride.

If he truly knows you and his heart is right, he will understand that it is only through your "undeserved kindness" (Romans 11:5[a]) that he can have a relationship with you at all.

Then he will have a story to tell! The story of how he has "received one blessing after another" because your "grace is not limited" (John 1:16[b])—it is entirely "free and undeserved" (Romans 11:6[c])!

May he always want to tell that story and "boast in" (2 Corinthians 10:17[d]) your wild, generous, uncontained love!

No one is as loving as you, Lord Jesus! May he live in love with you! May he always want to be where your people are, because you are always close to the humble, but you keep your "distance from the proud" (Psalm 138:6ᵉ).

"Oh, the joys of those who trust" in you, Lord, "who have no confidence in the proud" (Psalm 40:4ᶠ).

I ask that you will be his "confidence"; then you "will keep" him from "being caught" in so many traps (Proverbs 3:26ᵍ)!

Please keep him from the trap of materialism, the false god of our age. How easy it is for our hearts to be drawn to things that will never give satisfaction to our souls!

Your Word makes clear that "people who long to be rich fall into temptation and are trapped by many foolish and harmful desires that plunge them into ruin and destruction" (1 Timothy 6:9ʰ).

Please have mercy on him, so that his heart will not "envy sinners" and he will "always be zealous" for you (Proverbs 23:17)!

Please bless him with examples in faith that will encourage and inspire him, Lord Jesus. May he especially "follow the example" you have set for him (1 Corinthians 11:1)!

I also ask that you will give him grace so that he won't "be selfish" or "try to impress others." Please help him to genuinely "be humble," even "thinking of others as better" than himself (Philippians 2:3ⁱ).

If he does that, he will have the "same attitude that" you had (Philippians 2:5ʲ).

Then, he "will not be afraid on the day of judgment" and can even face you "with confidence" (1 John 4:17ᵏ), all because of your love that is at work in him.

On that day he will join the great shout of praise with all you have saved from sin and death, saying, "Not to us, O LORD, not to us, but to your name goes all the glory for your unfailing love and faithfulness" (Psalm 115:1[l])!

a NLT, b NIrV, c NLT, d ESV, e NLT, f NLT, g ESV, h NLT, i NLT, j NLT, k NLT, l NLT

ONE FOR THE TEAM

Love . . . is not arrogant or rude.
It does not insist on its own way.

1 Corinthians 13:4–5 (ESV)

He's just mentioned once in your Word, Father, but what is said about him is convicting: "Diotrephes . . . loves to be first" (3 John 9).

I'm afraid I know that feeling too well. But I thank you for teaching me that loving to be first isn't really love at all.

Your Word tells us to "love each other with genuine affection, and take delight in honoring each other" (Romans 12:10[a]).

I pray that my child will 'get' this, and find real pleasure in making others happy. Not for herself or whatever it may bring her . . . but simply out of love for you.

Your love transforms our hearts in such beautiful and unexpected ways. When we fall before you in weakness, you become "the strength" of our hearts. We belong to *you*, and then you let us call you *ours* "forever" (Psalm 73:26[b])!

You turn our focus inside out! Once we were stuck on ourselves, "gratifying the cravings of our sinful nature and following its desires and thoughts" (Ephesians 2:3). But once your Spirit begins to work within us you help us understand that only "you have the words that give eternal life" (John 6:68[c]).

You turn our hearts to loving and serving you. You even give us new love for others!

You are "pleased" when we "do good and share with others" (Hebrews 13:16), and I pray that my daughter will serve you in this way.

May she "see your face" (Psalm 17:15) reflected in the looks on others' faces as she attends to their needs with a heart full of faith. Yes, "make your face shine down" upon her, Lord (Psalm 80:3[d])!

I pray that my child will work well with others and be a team player. Please give her grace to learn how to cooperate with others while standing strong with you. Help her to be flexible and "not insist on" her "own way" (1 Corinthians 13:5[e]).

When she feels strongly about something I pray that you will help her to listen to others, because "pride only leads to arguing, but those who take advice are wise" (Proverbs 13:10[f]).

When others treat her unfairly, I ask that she will resist the temptation to "pay back one wrong act with another," and instead "always try to be kind" (1 Thessalonians 5:15[g]). May she have strength inside and "always be joyful" (1 Thessalonians 5:16[h]), raising a "shout of praise"

(Ezra 3:11) to you in her heart because of all you have done.

May she "never stop praying" (1 Thessalonians 5:17[i]), talking to you through the day about the specific circumstances of her life and recognizing your specific answers!

Those who cannot follow cannot lead. May she always "follow you" (Mark 10:28), led in the strength of your Spirit and your Word. Then she will kick the world's 'my way or the highway' attitude to the curb and humbly "walk with" (Revelation 3:4) you into the future you have planned!

a NLT, b ESV, c NLT, d NLT, e ESV, f NIrV, g NIrV, h NIrV, i NIrV

FAMILY RESEMBLANCE

Love . . . is not easily angered, it keeps no
record of wrongs.

1 Corinthians 13:4–5

I'm in awe of your forgiveness, Lord.

Even when you were being crucified, you called out, "Father,
forgive them, for they do not know what they are doing"
(Luke 23:34).

Your forgiveness is perfect. You don't even make us pay for
our sins; you "canceled the record of the charges against
us and took it away by nailing it to the cross" (Colossians 2:14[a]).

I praise you for what you've done for us! You "never sinned,"
but you became "the offering for our sin, so that we
could be made right with God" (2 Corinthians 5:21[b]).
Your forgiveness is beautiful, Lord. The most priceless
of all gifts!

But you also tell us that if we receive it, we have to give it away.

So much depends on this! You said that if we "refuse to
forgive others," the "Father will not forgive" our sins
(Matthew 6:15[c]).

I pray my child will understand this, Father, and will take it deeply and sincerely to heart. In those moments when she finds it difficult to forgive, I pray that she will ask you to help her so that your forgiveness can flow freely through her into the lives of others.

I remember Peter's question: "Lord, how often should I forgive someone who sins against me? Seven times?" (Matthew 18:21[d]).

"No, not seven times," you answered, "but seventy times seven!" (Matthew 18:22[e]). And then you reminded Peter of how we should always forgive from the heart because we've been forgiven so much.

How easily we forget this, Lord Jesus! Why is it we sometimes find it so hard to forgive?

Please give her the grace and strength she needs to do this, Lord.

No matter what wrongs may happen to her, I pray she will be able to let go of the past. I pray she will keep looking forward to you, "forgetting what is behind and straining toward what is ahead" (Philippians 3:13), obediently following your example in forgiveness and love.

Your Word tells us clearly, "Do not seek revenge or bear a grudge" (Leviticus 19:18). It also teaches that "wisdom yields patience," and it is to" our "glory to overlook an offense" (Proverbs 19:11).

Please help her to love so much that she "keeps no record of wrongs" (1 Corinthians 13:5), Lord Jesus.

You taught us, "Be merciful, even as your Father is merciful" (Luke 6:36[f]). You also said, "Love your enemies! Pray for those who persecute you! In that way, you will be acting as true children of your Father in heaven" (Matthew 5:44–45[g]).

Only you and equip her to do this, Lord, and I pray that you will! Then, when the Father looks on her in love, He'll see a distinct family resemblance.

Oh, He might not say 'She has my ears' or 'She has my nose.' He'll just say, 'She has my heart.'

a NLT, b NLT, c NLT, d NLT, e NLT, f ESV, g NLT

HIDE HERE

Love does not delight in evil but rejoices
with the truth. . . .
Oh, what joy for those whose disobedience is forgiven,
whose sin is put out of sight!
1 Corinthians 13:6; Psalm 32:1 (NLT)

I know there will be times when my child needs to repent,
Lord.

Sin sticks its bony finger into our lives and points us in the
wrong direction, away from you and all that is good.

So I send this prayer ahead to help show him the way home.

You are our hearts' true home, where we were meant to be
all along. But sin makes us run from you, Lord God, just
as it caused Adam and Eve to hide themselves "among
the trees of the garden" (Genesis 3:8ᵃ).

So today I pray that when my child has sinned, his heart
will be moved to turn *from* sin and *toward* you.

May he be drawn to your goodness and understand that
there can be no lasting joy apart from you.

I think of what David realized when he persisted in sinning: "When I refused to confess my sin my body wasted away and I groaned all day long" (Psalm 32:3[b]).

So many grow so old so young! Their sins weigh them down, and they "refuse to come to" you to "have life" (John 5:40).

But "oh, what joy for those whose disobedience is forgiven, whose sin is put out of sight!" (Psalm 32:1[c]).

"What joy for those whose record" you have "cleared of guilt, whose lives are lived in complete honesty" (Psalm 32:2[d]) and openness before you!

I pray that your perfect love will fill my child's life so that he will "not delight in evil" (1 Corinthians 13:6).

Whenever he sins may he be quick "to repent" (Acts 17:30[e]) and be sincere in it! Give him a sense of conviction and urgency like David had when he wrote, "Let all the godly pray to you while there is still time" (Psalm 32:6[f]).

I pray he will "return" to you, understanding that you are "merciful and compassionate, slow to get angry and filled with unfailing love." You are "eager to relent and not punish" (Joel 2:13[g])!

May he run to you, sick of sin and longing for something better! May the cry of his heart be, "You are my hiding place; you protect me from trouble. You surround me with songs of victory" (Psalm 32:7[h])!

Even when we bring trouble on ourselves, you love us still. Even when we are "overwhelmed by our sins, you forgive them all" (Psalm 65:3[i]) and give us victory over them as we turn to you.

"Many sorrows come to the wicked, but unfailing love surrounds those who trust" in you (Psalm 32:10[j]).

May your "kindness and faithfulness" be with him, Lord (2 Samuel 15:20)! May he "run to you to hide" him (Psalm 143:9[k]), so he may be forever safe in your love.

a ESV, b NLT, c NLT, d NLT, e ESV, f NLT, g NLT, h NLT, i NLT, j NLT, k NLT

OUCH!

Love never gives up, never loses faith, is always hopeful, and endures through every circumstance.

1 Corinthians 13:7 (NLT)

Sometimes I think about things that have happened to my child and I think, 'Ouch! That had to hurt!'

Vaccinations, cuts and scrapes and splinters, even words . . . The world is so hard and we are soft by comparison.

I understand that some hurts are necessary. They help us learn and serve to make us stronger.

But I praise you that there is something that makes us stronger still: your love!

Your love is stronger than all the world's hurts. "Who shall separate us from the love of Christ? Shall trouble or hardship or persecution or famine or nakedness or danger or sword?" (Romans 8:35).

Nothing can, and nothing will! We are "more than conquerors" through you "who loved us" (Romans 8:37a)!

"It is good for the heart to be strengthened by grace" (Hebrews 13:9[b]), and today I pray that my child will be strong and brave in your love.

Hurts of the body and hurts of the heart may come, but "we know that in all things" you work "for the good of those who love" you, "who have been called" according to your "purpose" (Romans 8:28).

The purposes of your heart—to save and to love—stand firm "through all generations" (Psalm 33:11), and I pray that this child you have given me will always believe in you!

I ask that you will help him to stay "hopeful" and hang on to your love "through every circumstance" (1 Corinthians 13:7[c]).

Help him to trust you, because the end of every matter is in your hands—and if he is patient, he will discover that you always show yourself faithful.

You waste nothing! You are even able to take that which the adversary means for "evil" in our lives and turn it "for good" (Genesis 50:20[d])!

David saw many difficulties in life, but he prayed, "I remain confident of this: I will see the goodness of the LORD in the land of the living" (Psalm 27:13). May my child join him in that prayer and "live by faith" (Galatians 3:11[e])!

I pray that he will "give" his "burdens" to you, so that you "will take care" of him. You "will not permit the godly to slip and fall" (Psalm 55:22[f]).

"The best-equipped army cannot save a king," but you watch "over those who fear" you, "those who rely on" your "unfailing love" (Psalm 33:16, 18[g]).

When this world causes him hurt, I pray he will take comfort in you. Then he will know that you are with him, and you are "mighty enough to save"! You "take great delight" in him and will "calm" him in your "love." You even "sing with joy" over us (Zephaniah 3:17[h])!

Oh, I pray he will hear your song, Lord, and take it to heart. Then, healed of his hurts, he will "dance with the joyful" before you (Jeremiah 31:4)!

a ESV, b ESV, c NLT, d NKJV, e ESV, f NLT, g NLT, h NIrV

FACE-TO-FACE WITH LOVE

Love never fails. . . . And now these three
remain: faith, hope and love. But the
greatest of these is love.

1 Corinthians 13:8, 13

When my child was just a baby she would study my face with wide-eyed wonder.

Words were unnecessary. Just the simple, loving look that passed between us was enough.

Sometimes I wonder if heaven will be a little like that, Father.

We will have returned to innocence, "without a spot or wrinkle or any other blemish" (Ephesians 5:27ᵃ), every sin washed clean through "the precious blood" of your Son (1 Peter 1:19ᵇ).

"Then we shall see" you clearly, even "face to face" (1 Corinthians 13:12)!

We will look on you in love and wonder, and words will be insufficient to describe all that you are.

"How great you are, O Sovereign LORD! There is no one like you, and there is no God but you" (2 Samuel 7:22).

Each day we will see something new and wonderful, and we will worship you tirelessly forever, because "strength and joy fill" the place where you are (1 Chronicles 16:27ᶜ). "Yours, LORD, is the greatness and the power and the glory and the majesty and the splendor" (1 Chronicles 29:11)!

Your love is the greatest thing in our lives, and I pray that the gift of your love will be my child's most prized possession.

I ask that you bless my child with a special sensitivity to your presence so that she will never want to be far from you. "Let no sin rule over" her, Lord (Psalm 119:133)!

I pray that she will always "follow the way of love" (1 Corinthians 14:1) and never "turn from your path" (Isaiah 63:17ᵈ).

But if her "foot slips," may "your mercy" meet her and "hold" her up (Psalm 94:18ᶜ)!

You take care of your "flock like a shepherd," and you gather "the lambs" in your "arms" and carry them "close" to your "heart" (Isaiah 40:11). She is my lamb, Lord, and I pray she will be yours as well.

If you carry her close to your heart, she'll be able to look up and know that "your face" shines upon her (Psalm 80:7), no matter what she goes through. And even when she isn't able to see your face, she'll be able to 'hear' and trust your heart.

If she can know and trust that you love her and are carrying her, she can go through anything—because your "love never fails" (1 Corinthians 13:8).

No matter how the adversary may try to come after her, your "purpose will stand," and you "will do all" that you "please" (Isaiah 46:10).

"Sovereign Lord," you are our "strong deliverer" (Psalm 140:7). You "pour out your unfailing love on those who love you" (Psalm 36:10^f)!

"Let your unfailing love surround" her, Lord, for her "hope is in you alone" (Psalm 33:22^g).

I pray she will have "faith" and "hope" (1 Corinthians 13:13) in you as long as she lives, and will live to love you forever!

a NLT, b ESV, c NLT, d NLT, e NKJV, f NLT, g NLT

Week 5

PROTECTED

Uncle Abraham, Armor, and Angels

To Him who tucks me into bed,
please station angels around his head,
and guard my child wherever he be,
and bring him back, dear Lord, to Thee.

Robert J. Morgan

Abraham's nephew Lot didn't make the best choices. When Abraham offered him any land he wanted, Lot chose "the fertile plains of the Jordan Valley" (Genesis 13:10 NLT). The land was productive and beautiful, "but the people of this area were extremely wicked and constantly sinned against the LORD" (Genesis 13:13 NLT). Lot probably knew that, but still chose to move his entire family and settle near Sodom.

It wasn't long before he'd regret his decision. Marauders captured Lot "and carried off everything he owned" (Genesis 14:12 NLT). But even after his Uncle Abraham rescued him, Lot returned to Sodom. And this time, he moved into the city itself. Lot was sitting at the city gates, a place of prominence, when God sent angels to destroy Sodom.

You have to wonder what compromises Lot made along the way to become a prominent citizen of Sodom. When the men of the city want to assault Lot's angelic guests, he called the men "brothers" and offered them his daughters instead (Genesis 19:7–8). Then, when the angels told him to leave because the city was about to be wiped out, Lot "still hesitated" (Genesis 19:16 NLT).

But "the Lord was merciful" in spite of Lot's terrible choices. "The angels *seized* his hand and the hands of his wife and two daughters and rushed them to safety outside the city" (Genesis 19:6 NLT, italics added). Why? Because someone was praying for Lot. Genesis 19:29 (NLT) makes this clear: "But God had listened to Abraham's request and kept Lot safe, removing him from the disaster that engulfed the cities on the plain."

As the parent of a former prodigal, I love those verses. They show me how God intervened powerfully in the life of someone who was making bad choices. That intervention was the result of God's kindness in answering prayer. He even sent His angels to take Lot by the hand and pull him out of harm's way. And it might not have happened if Abraham hadn't asked.

This week we're asking for every piece of "the full armor of God" for our sons and daughters. Our children need us to pray for their protection so they may "be strong in the Lord and his mighty power," and be able to take their stand "against the devil's schemes" (Ephesians 6:10–11).

These are prayers that our children may stand in the strength that only God can give, and praise Him for His life and soul-saving mercy forever.

SOUL ARMOR

Put on the full armor of God so that you
can take your stand against the devil's
schemes. . . . Stand firm then, with the belt
of truth buckled around your waist.

Ephesians 6:11, 14

"May your love and truth always keep" my child "safe,"
Father (Psalm 40:11ᵃ).

Your Word is very clear on the fact that our "adversary the
devil walks about like a roaring lion, seeking whom he
may devour" (1 Peter 5:8ᵇ). I pray my son will "resist
him, standing firm in the faith" (1 Peter 5:9).

To do that he needs armor for his soul that only you can
give. I pray your truth will wrap around him and hold
him secure, Lord.

He needs your truth to fill his mind and heart, and "your
word is truth" (John 17:17ᶜ). You "speak the truth" and
"declare what is right" (Isaiah 45:19ᵈ).

Because "you delight in truth in the inward being" (Psalm
51:6ᵉ), I pray he will love your Word and take it to heart.

Let your Word enter his mind again and again as he goes through the day. May "the word of Christ dwell" in him "richly" (Colossians 3:16[f])!

In this cynical world that asks, "What is truth?" (John 18:38[g]), I ask that he "will know the truth" of your teaching, so that "the truth will set" him "free" (John 8:32[h])—free to really live for you and know the joy you alone can give, Lord Jesus!

I pray he will be, like you, a "man of truth" with "nothing false about him" (John 7:18).

"May integrity and honesty protect" him, because he put his "hope in you" (Psalm 25:21[i]).

I also ask that he will be a man who tells the truth when it isn't to his own advantage, and who keeps his promises "even when it hurts" (Psalm 15:4[j]).

Give him insight to see through this world's toxic fog, the deception that says whatever he believes is okay as long as it makes him happy. Only *you* lead to lasting happiness, and I pray he will understand this!

May he humbly embrace the beauty of your saving truth with all his heart. May he speak "the truth from his heart" (Psalm 15:2[k]) because you are in his heart and he consciously lives in your presence.

When the adversary tries to undermine your truth in his heart, I ask that you will fill him with your Spirit. Your Spirit is "the Spirit of truth" whom "the world cannot receive, because it neither sees him nor knows him." But I pray my son will "know him," because "he dwells with" him "and will be in" him (John 14:17[l]).

May he be "firmly established in the truth" (2 Peter 1:12) of all you are, Lord!

"I have no greater joy" than to hear that my son is "walking in the truth" (3 John 4). Come what may, he will always be safe there—because he is walking with you!

a NIrV, b NKJV, c ESV, d ESV, e ESV, f ESV, g ESV, h NLT, i NLT, j NLT, k NIrV, l ESV

WRAPPED IN RIGHTEOUSNESS

> . . . with the breastplate of righteousness in
> place.
>
> Ephesians 6:14

Righteousness is such a challenging thing, Lord.

"What is man . . . that he can be righteous?" (Job 15:14ᵃ).

When we make even the slightest progress in righteousness, we're so easily tempted to pride ourselves on it.
Yet "pride goes before destruction, and a haughty spirit
before a fall" (Proverbs 16:18ᵇ).

Your Word makes this clear when it tells us, "Look at the
proud! They trust in themselves, and their lives are
crooked. But the righteous will live by their faithfulness" to you (Habakkuk 2:4ᶜ).

How can we be righteous without being righteous in our
own eyes?

Only through you. You alone are truly righteous. You are
"the LORD our righteousness" (Jeremiah 23:6ᵈ)!

So today I pray my daughter will wear "the breastplate of
righteousness" (Ephesians 6:14) and wear it right. I pray
that she will borrow yours.

She can only do that if you put it on her. She needs "a righteousness" that none of us could ever achieve on our own. She needs "that which comes through faith" in you, Lord Jesus: "the righteousness from God that depends on faith" (Philippians 3:9[e]). Only a "righteousness that is by faith from first to last" (Romans 1:17) will give her the full protection she needs!

Loving Savior, you have become "our righteousness, holiness and redemption" (1 Corinthians 1:30). I pray my daughter will be protected from spiritual harm by staying so close to you that you that she is completely surrounded by your love. "The promise of life" is in you (2 Timothy 1:1[f])!

I ask that she will worship you wholeheartedly with the strength only you can give, and completely "rely on" what you have done for her, putting "no confidence in human effort" (Philippians 3:3[g]).

Then you, and only you, will be all the answer needed to the one "who accuses" her "day and night" (Revelation 12:10). "The body armor" of your righteousness (Ephesians 6:14[h]) will protect her completely!

Thank you for speaking "to the Father for us" (1 John 2:1[i]), Lord Jesus!

I praise you for your priceless righteousness! And I ask that you give my daughter the wisdom to understand that obedience to you is the only response we can give for all of your goodness to us.

If she comprehends that, one day you'll replace the beautiful, shining body armor you have given her with "fine linen, bright and pure," linen that represents "the righteous deeds of the saints" (Revelation 19:8[j]).

Then, safe and sound at last with the battle won, she will
find herself before you in indescribable love and joy, at
"the wedding feast of the Lamb" (Revelation 19:7[k]).

a ESV, b ESV, c NLT, d NASB, e ESV, f ESV, g NLT, h NLT, i NIrV, j ESV, k NLT

NEW SHOES!

For shoes, put on the peace that comes
from the Good News so that you will be
fully prepared.

Ephesians 6:15 (NLT)

Today I'd like to ask for beautiful feet for my child.

Your Word says, "How beautiful are the feet of those who bring good news!" (Romans 10:15). I pray he will carry your good news wherever he goes! I ask that my son will love you so much that he will be compelled to share you with others in the things he does and says.

I pray that your peace will rest upon him so deeply and so completely that he will "always be prepared to give an answer to everyone who asks" him to "give the reason for the hope" that he has, and that he will "do this with gentleness and respect" (1 Peter 3:15).

There was a time in his life when he got so excited about shoes. He believed new shoes could help him run faster and jump higher. He put such faith in them! Today I pray that he will have faith in you so that your strength "powerfully works" (Colossians 1:29) through him.

I pray he will be someone that you will be pleased with, a man who takes your interests to heart above his own. Isn't that what a servant does?

I ask that he serve you so well that he will one day hear you say, "Well done, good and faithful servant! You have been faithful with a few things; I will put you in charge of many things. Come and share your master's happiness!" (Matthew 25:23).

If he walks in your peace ready to serve you, he will always be "safe in" your "love" (Jude 21ᵃ).

I pray that he will stay on your path, and "not swerve to the right or the left," so that you keep his "foot away from evil" (Proverbs 4:27ᵇ).

You came to "guide our feet into the path of peace" (Luke 1:79)—may he always follow you on it!

I ask that he "pursue righteousness and a godly life, along with faith, love, perseverance, and gentleness" (1 Timothy 6:11ᶜ).

May the good news of all you are and the peace of your presence carry him to new places of grace and understanding.

I pray that my son will know the joy of sharing you with others and personally witness your amazing power to transform hearts and lives.

May you move through him to "say to the captives, 'Come out,' and to those in darkness, 'Be free!'" (Isaiah 49:9).

And may he watch in wordless wonder as it happens—as chains break and light falls on faces as hearts turn to you, "God our Savior . . . the hope of everyone on earth" (Psalm 65:5ᵈ)!

a NLT, b ESV, c NLT, d NLT

Day 32

WHEN BELIEVING IS SEEING

In addition to all this, take up the shield of
faith, with which you can extinguish all the
flaming arrows of the evil one.

Ephesians 6:16

Today I pray that my child will pick up the shield of faith
and use it well.

I see it in her hands now, a strong shield emblazoned with
"the Lion of the tribe of Judah" who "has triumphed"
(Revelation 5:5).

She is but a lamb, but she is your lamb, Lord Jesus—and
she conquers! "This is the victory that has overcome the
world—our faith" (1 John 5:4ª).

So by faith I bring her before you today, and by faith I see
her standing strong through your mercy.

Yet I know she is not the only one standing there. There is
an adversary, dark and menacing. His eye is keen and
his flaming arrow flies straight at her weakness.

But it misses! In wisdom quicker than thought, your Spirit
speaks to her and she obeys—the shield flashes! The
arrow glances away and falls broken to the ground.

My child lives! Just as you promised. You said, "Because I live, you will live also" (John 14:19[b]).

I praise you for watching over us, Lord. You stand "beside" us "like a great warrior" (Jeremiah 20:11[c]), and I pray for your protection for my child as long as she must "fight the good fight" of faith (1 Timothy 6:12[d]).

May "your compassion come speedily to meet" her (Psalm 79:8[e]) in every need. Through faith in you she can "extinguish all the flaming arrows of the evil one" (Ephesians 6:14), regardless of how many are aimed at her.

Strong Savior, you promise such beautiful things to those who believe. You said, "I have come as a light to shine in this dark world, so that all who put their trust in me will no longer remain in the dark" (John 12:46[f]).

Let the "light of life" (Job 33:30[g]) shine on her, Lord!

You said, "Anyone who believes in me will live, even after dying" (John 11:25[h]). You even told us, "Anyone who believes has *eternal* life" (John 6:47[i]).

So I pray she will believe with faith that lasts—a loving, living faith in you!

You "gave" yourself for her "to redeem" her (Titus 2:14[j]) and set her free "from the power of darkness" (Colossians 1:13[k]).

Your Word assures us that "everyone who believes" in you "receives forgiveness of sins" through your "name" (Acts 10:43[l]). I praise you for this gift beyond price that you secured for us at the cross!

May she "live by faith, not by sight" (2 Corinthians 5:7) as she trusts you to be faithful all of her life on this earth, and beyond!

May she have "the assurance of things hoped for" and "the conviction of things not seen" (Hebrews 11:1[m])—before they even occur—because she "can confidently say, 'The Lord is my helper'" (Hebrews 13:6[n])!

"All things are possible for the one who believes" (Mark 9:23[o]), because the One she believes in is *you!*

a ESV, b NKJV, c NLT, d ESV, e ESV, f NLT, g ESV, h NLT, i NLT *italics added*, j ESV, k NKJV, l ESV, m ESV, n ESV, o ESV

HELMET OF HOPE

And take the helmet of salvation.

Ephesians 6:17 (ESV)

Today as I pray that my child will be "protected by the armor of faith and love," I ask that you will help him put on as a helmet, "the confidence of our salvation" (1 Thessalonians 5:8ᵃ).

He needs this because our adversary the devil is a predator and "the father of lies" (John 8:44). "When anyone hears the message about the kingdom and does not understand it, the evil one comes and snatches away what was sown in their heart" (Matthew 13:19).

So I ask that you fill my son with an extra measure of "spiritual wisdom and understanding" (Colossians 1:9ᵇ) about your will for him as a believer.

I pray that he will "be on guard" and "stand firm in the faith," and that he will learn to "be courageous" and "strong" (1 Corinthians 16:13ᶜ).

When the devil tries to assault his mind and attack what he believes, I ask that he will keep his "head in all situations" (2 Timothy 4:5).

May there be no doubt in his mind that you have saved him, and may he be enthusiastically thankful for "such a great salvation" (Hebrews 2:3[d])!

Just as Abraham "believed" you and was called your "friend" (James 2:23[e]), I pray my son will have a deep and personal relationship with you that will continue to grow as long as he lives.

Then he will "not lose heart" regardless of his external circumstances, because "inwardly" he is "being renewed day by day" (2 Corinthians 4:16).

Then he will be able to say with great confidence, "I know the one in whom I trust, and I am sure that he is able to guard what I have entrusted to him until the day of his return" (2 Timothy 1:12[f]).

I ask that you will so assure him of his faith that he will be able to pray, "You have been my hope, Sovereign LORD," and "my confidence since my youth" (Psalm 71:5).

I ask that he will be so protected in your armor that he will be able to enter the battle with courage—not simply on the defensive, but taking it to the enemy!

You have promised, Lord Jesus, that "the gates of hell shall not prevail" against your church (Matthew 16:18[g]).

I ask that he will be so strong in you and in your "mighty power" (Ephesians 6:10) that he will join your church in the assault on those gates—and the sheer force of your strength in him will cause the gates to shudder and shatter so that captives are set free!

I pray my son will "be active in sharing" his faith, so that he "will completely understand every good thing we have" in you (Philemon 6[h]).

Then he will love you "even though" he has "never seen" you, and as he trusts you he will "rejoice with a glorious, inexpressible joy." And "the reward for trusting" you will be "the salvation" of his soul! (1 Peter 1:8–9[i]).

May "the hope laid up" for him "in heaven" protect him as long as he lives (Colossians 1:5[j]), so that he lives to praise you forever!

a NLT, b NIrV, c NLT, d ESV, e ESV, f NLT, g ESV, h NIrV, i NLT, j ESV

PROTECTED BY YOUR WORD

Take . . . the sword of the Spirit, which is
the word of God.

Ephesians 6:17

Thank you for your Word, Father.

"All Scripture is inspired" by you, "and is useful to teach us
what is true and to make us realize what is wrong in our
lives. It corrects us when we are wrong and teaches us to
do what is right" (2 Timothy 3:16[a]).

Today I pray the power of your Word over my child's life.

You use your Word "to prepare and equip" us "to do every
good work" (2 Timothy 3:17[b]). May your Word make
him effective for you!

I pray that the wisdom of your Word will protect my child
as long as he lives.

Lord Jesus, every time the devil tried to tempt you in the
wilderness you answered, "It is written . . ." (Matthew
4:4, 4:7, 4:10[c]).

When the adversary tries to lead my child astray, I ask that
you will help him to find his answer and "way of escape"
(1 Corinthians 10:13[d]) in what is written in your Word.

I pray that your Word will be "hidden" in his heart so he "might not sin against you" (Psalm 119:11).

Let your Word protect him! Guide his steps "by your word," so he "will not be overcome by evil" (Psalm 119:133[e]).

Your Word "is alive and powerful. It is sharper than the sharpest two-edged sword, cutting between soul and spirit, between joint and marrow" (Hebrews 4:12[f]).

I ask that my son will be a man "who correctly handles the word of truth" (2 Timothy 2:15). May he share your Word humbly and yet powerfully with others!

When the world around him insists on going its own way, I pray he will not "wander from the truth" (James 5:19) or "neglect your word" (Psalm 119:16), but will instead firmly stand on it. Please help him not to be "be wise" in his own "estimation" (Romans 12:16[g]) or to value contemporary thinking or trends over your eternal truth.

I pray he will learn to respect your Word and even "stand in awe" of it (Psalm 119:120[h]). May he place himself under your Word and not over it!

May your Word give him wisdom and discernment for living so that he can say, "How I love your instructions! I think about them all day long" (Psalm 119:97[i]).

Your Spirit speaks through your Word unlike anywhere else. I ask that he will long to spend time with you there, to hear your voice, and know the comfort only you can give him.

I pray "your word" will be his "source of hope" (Psalm 119:114[j]), and a refreshing place of encouragement that he will run to again and again.

Open his eyes "to see the wonderful truths in your instructions" (Psalm 119:18ᵏ), Lord! May your Word be his
"treasure" and his "heart's delight" (Psalm 119:111ˡ)!

"Heaven and earth will pass away," but your words "will
never pass away" (Mark 13:31).

Lifted by your "Spirit of truth" (John 15:26ᵐ), may his heart
leap from the page to the peace of your perfect presence!

a NLT, b NLT, c ESV, d NASB, e NLT, f NLT, g NASB, h NLT, i NLT, j NLT, k NLT, l NLT, m ESV

Day 35

ARMORED WITH PRAYER

And pray in the Spirit on all occasions
with all kinds of prayers and requests. With
this in mind, be alert and always keep on
praying for all the Lord's people.

Ephesians 6:18

I ask that my child will discover your amazing power to answer prayer, Lord. Her armor isn't complete without it!

Prayer isn't just part of her armor—it's a weapon too!

"The weapons we fight with are not the weapons of the world. On the contrary, they have divine power to demolish strongholds" (2 Corinthians 10:4).

Please help my daughter to comprehend the amazing power that's available to her when she prays. You allow our prayers to move your "mighty hand" (1 Kings 8:42ᵃ)!

I also ask you to give my daughter the grace to understand that you have ordained that some things will happen "only by prayer" (Mark 9:29).

You are just waiting for us to pray! You told your people once, "Call to me and I will answer you and tell you great and unsearchable things you do not know" (Jeremiah 33:3).

I pray that she will call on you! Help her to "devote" herself "to prayer with an alert mind and a thankful heart" (Colossians 4:2[b]).

I pray that prayer won't be a 'last resort' in her life. Let it be a 'first'!

May she call on your name "every day," and "spread out" her "hands to you" (Psalm 88:9). And may she have the assurance that "as soon as" you hear, you "will answer" (Isaiah 30:19)!

I thank you that you don't always give us what we ask for—you measure each request through your perfect, loving wisdom.

When answers don't come in the way she may want, please help her to understand that you are "a faithful God," and "those who wait" for your help are always "blessed" (Isaiah 30:18[c]).

How blessed we are to have this privilege of prayer, Lord Jesus! Thank you for opening a "new and living way" (Hebrews 10:20[d]) into the very presence of the Father!

I praise you that we can "have confidence to enter the most Holy Place" (Hebrews 10:19) through your blood shed for us on the cross.

Thank you that we can "come boldly to the throne of grace" and "obtain mercy and find grace to help in time of need" (Hebrews 4:16[e]).

May the cry of her heart always be, "I call to God, and the LORD saves me" (Psalm 55:16).

May she "pray in the Spirit on all occasions with all kinds of prayers and requests" (Ephesians 6:18), so that she may discover the wonder of what you alone can do.

And with that in mind, I also ask that you will give me grace to "always keep on praying" (Ephesians 6:18) for her!

a ESV, b NLT, c NLT, d ESV, e NKJV

Week 6

FAITHFUL

Gabriel's Lesson

> God brings His purposes to pass in spite of
> all men may do, and often through what
> they do, and He will utilize the very things
> which look as if they were going dead
> against their fulfillment; God goes steadily
> on and involves us in the fulfillment.
>
> Oswald Chambers

It's a lesson in prayer from the mouth of an angel, and it comes when you least expect it.

Elizabeth and Zechariah had prayed for a baby for years. But year after year, the prayer seemed to go unanswered. Or maybe God's answer was "No."

Some began to wonder why. Having no children was a "disgrace" in their opinion (Luke 1:25), a sign that someone had displeased God. So neighbors and "friends" began to speculate that maybe God was judging Elizabeth and Zechariah for some secret sin.

The years went by until Zechariah and Elizabeth "were both very old" (Luke 1:7 NLT). One day, Zechariah was on duty in the temple. He was standing alone in the sanctuary when none other than the archangel Gabriel appeared.

The old man was terrified, but Gabriel told him, "Don't be afraid, Zechariah! God has heard your prayer. Your wife, Elizabeth, will give you a son, and you are to name him John. You will have great joy and gladness, and many will rejoice at his birth, for he will be great in the eyes of the Lord" (Luke 1:13–15 NLT).

There it is, Gabriel's lesson. Did you catch it? Like so many things that angels do, it happened so quickly it's easy to miss. The lesson is found in five little words: *God has heard your prayer.*

If you're Zechariah, you might be wondering, *What prayer?* Elizabeth's childbearing years were long past, and by this time it's doubtful Zechariah had in mind the answer to a request made decades earlier.

But as soon as Gabriel saw Zechariah, that was one of the first things out of his mouth. And there's comfort in that for every praying parent.

God's timing is rarely our own, but it is always perfect. We may ask for good things for our children—things that we know God would want us to pray for—but we don't always see good things happening. That doesn't mean blessings won't come. We can still trust that good will occur, even if we don't know how or when. Our part is to rest and trust in God, knowing that He is faithful to remember our prayers even if we made them years earlier.

Sometimes God doesn't give us what we seek *when* we ask for it because He's waiting to give us something better.

Zechariah and Elizabeth longed for a son—but God gave them a prophet. And not just any prophet. They got a man with "the spirit and power of Elijah" (Luke 1:17)—the very one who would announce the Messiah.

The pages to come are filled with prayers that our children will have faith in God and discover His faithfulness for themselves. There are practical prayers about confidence in God, personal integrity, the meaning of true success, obedience, "moving mountains," and more.

As you pray these prayers, I hope you'll take "Gabriel's lesson" to heart. God hears our prayers! Zechariah and Elizabeth may have lost faith that their prayers would ever be answered. But God didn't. He was only taking His own perfect time, preparing a miracle.

MUSTARD SEEDS, MOUNTAINS, AND PROMISED LANDS

> "I tell you the truth, if you had faith even as small as a mustard seed, you could say to this mountain, 'Move from here to there,' and it would move. Nothing would be impossible."
>
> Matthew 17:20 (NLT)

Sometimes my child will have to face mountains.

So today I pray for those faith-building moments in his life when he must choose to "trust in" you (Psalm 115:9ᵃ).

I'm reminded of Joshua and Caleb. When Moses sent a team to scout out the land you promised to your people, Joshua and Caleb were the only ones who believed they could go in, regardless of the obstacles. They told the people not to "be afraid," and assured them the Lord was with them (Numbers 14:9).

But the people didn't believe. And because they didn't, you said "not one of them will ever see the land I promised" (Numbers 14:23). Only Joshua and Caleb got to go in.

I never want my son to miss out on what you've promised, Lord!

Help me to do my part to "see to it" that my child does not have "a sinful, unbelieving heart that turns away" from you, "the living God" (Hebrews 3:12).

Even if others are doubting around him, I ask that you give him a "different spirit" so that he believes and "follows" you "wholeheartedly" (Numbers 14:24). I pray he will enter into many 'promised lands,' those special places you have waiting for him because he believes in you.

You are "a rewarder of those who diligently seek" you (Hebrews 11:6[b])!

No matter what obstacles may stand before him, in your presence "the mountains quake, and the hills melt away" (Nahum 1:5[c]).

So I pray he will stand with you. As long as his faith is in you, "nothing will be impossible" (Matthew 17:20[d]).

Even a little faith—just 'a mustard seed'—is a powerful thing when it's placed in your hands.

Help him to look beyond life's challenges and see you. Please give him faith to understand that you are greater than anything he faces!

I pray he will walk so closely with you that he will have the "confidence" only you can give him, quietly assured that you will answer his prayers because he's asking "according to" your will (1 John 5:14).

You are "the great God, the mighty and awesome God" (Deuteronomy 10:17[e]) who works miracles! You are "the only one who is worthy" of praise (Deuteronomy 10:21[f]).

I pray that my son will learn the personal discipline of praising you often. The more he praises you, the more his faith will grow.

Like Peter walking "on the water" (Matthew 14:29[g]), when he puts his eyes on you he will really go places!

a ESV, b NKJV, c NLT, d ESV, e NLT, f NLT, g ESV

"YOU CAN DO IT!"

Then Moses said, "If you don't personally
go with us,
don't make us leave this place. How will
anyone know
that you look favorably on me—on me
and on your people—
if you don't go with us? . . . The LORD replied
to Moses,
"I will indeed do what you have asked, for
I look favorably on you,
and I know you by name."

Exodus 33:15–17 (NLT)

How you honored Moses, Lord.

He was one of the greatest people who ever lived, given a
permanent place in history for leading your people.

Your Word tells us what made him great, and the reason
you singled him out: "Moses was a very humble man,
more humble than anyone else on the face of the earth"
(Numbers 12:3).

Moses had the confidence to lead an entire nation out of slavery against incredible odds because his confidence wasn't in himself. It was in you.

I ask for the same kind of confidence for my child, Lord.

Whatever challenges he may face in life, I pray he will "not be afraid or discouraged," because he understands that "the battle" is not his, but yours (2 Chronicles 20:15).

This can only happen if he lives for you and walks with you.

So I pray he will live in such a way that you "look favorably on" him. Like Moses, may he hear your voice quietly assuring him, "I know you by name" (Exodus 3:17[a]).

I pray for great faith in my child's life, a faith that is unusually strong because of his closeness to you, a faith with the vision to grasp that "what is impossible with man is possible with God" (Luke 18:27[b]).

"Through faith" in you, Lord Jesus, "we may approach God with freedom and confidence" (Ephesians 3:12). And I praise you that we can!

I pray you will "personally go with" him (Exodus 33:15[c]) wherever he goes, and that he will live in the strength of a humble awareness of your presence.

How blessed we are when we know you are near and our thoughts are filled with you!

I pray he will listen for your voice, longing for what pleases you most of all. When the world tells him your work and your will can't be done, may he hear you say, 'You can do it!'

Your Word makes clear that "those who trust their own insight are foolish" (Proverbs 28:26[d]). But if we trust in you, all will be well, come what may.

"Such confidence" is ours through you, Lord Jesus, because "our competence comes from God" (2 Corinthians 3:4–5).

I pray he will live a righteous and faithful life in you. Then "the fruit of righteousness will be peace" in his heart before you, and "its effect will be quietness and confidence forever" (Isaiah 32:17).

"Nothing is too hard for you" (Jeremiah 32:17[e])! You are "El-Shaddai—'God Almighty'" (Genesis 35:11[f])!

If he holds on to "confidence" in you, he "will be richly rewarded" (Hebrews 10:35)!

a NLT, b ESV, c NLT, d NLT, e ESV, f NLT

Day 38

WORK OF YOUR HANDS

"The Lord has filled Bezalel with the Spirit
of God,
giving him great wisdom, ability, and
expertise
in all kinds of crafts. He is a master
craftsman."

Exodus 35:31–32 (NLT)

What is it you want my child to do, Lord?

Samuel was young when you called him. So was David. And John the Baptist hadn't even been born (see Luke 1:5–25)!

Still your Spirit was at work in them, shaping and molding them to accomplish just what you wanted them to accomplish in life.

I pray this for my child as well, Father. I ask that you will use me to encourage him in his life's work, whatever it may be.

But here I know I also have to be careful not to force my will or my way. "We can make our plans," but you determine "our steps" (Proverbs 16:9ᵃ).

May "your will be done" (Matthew 6:10) in his life and work!

I pray he will follow you into whatever work you have planned for him.

When he is still trying to determine what he should do, I pray he will "ask" you "for guidance" (Isaiah 8:19ᵇ), and that you will make the way so clear he cannot miss it!

Please also give him the wisdom to understand that his work is a calling and gift from you. "Whatever" he does, I pray that he will "work at it with all" his "heart," as someone "working for" you (Colossians 3:23), not for himself.

May his work be *your* work, Lord! May your hand be on him so that you are moving through him to accomplish good things!

Please bless him in his work, Lord! Just as you were "with Joseph, and gave him success in whatever he did" (Genesis 39:23), I pray that you will show favor to my child.

But I also ask that he "would never say" to himself, "'I have achieved this wealth with my own strength and energy'" (Deuteronomy 8:17ᶜ).

Please give him the grace to humbly understand that you are "the one who gives" us "power to be successful" (Deuteronomy 8:18ᵈ). Any ability or intelligence we have—including the strength to apply it—is simply a gift from you.

Please keep him from the idolatry of self and things, Father!

May he comprehend that money is your tool in his hands to further your work and bless others. I pray he will know the joy of bringing "the whole tithe" into your house, so you will "throw open the floodgates of heaven and pour out so much blessing that there will not be room enough to store it" (Malachi 3:10).

May he use his "worldly resources to benefit others" (Luke 16:19[e]), so that they may know you.

And when his work on this earth is completed, I pray he will hear you say, "Well done, good and faithful servant! You have been faithful with a few things; I will put you in charge of many things. Come and share your master's happiness!'" (Matthew 25:23).

a NLT, b NLT, c NLT, d NLT, e NLT

WHEN NO ONE IS LOOKING

> Remember, the sins of some people are
> obvious, leading them to certain judg-
> ment. But there are others whose sins
> will not be revealed until later. In the same
> way, the good deeds of some people are
> obvious. And the good deeds done
> in secret will someday come to light.
>
> 1 Timothy 5:24–25 (NLT)

I pray that my child will have the integrity to do what is right when she knows no one is looking.

You are always watching, Father! You see us when we think no one does.

We "can never escape from your Spirit!" We "can never get away from your presence!" (Psalm 139:7ᵃ).

"You spread out our sins before you—our secret sins—and you see them all" (Psalm 90:8ᵇ).

But because you see all of "what is done in secret," you also "reward" us when we are faithful to you (Matthew 6:4). I pray that she will be!

I ask that you will continually remind my child of your presence so she may be comforted and encouraged when she is alone.

I pray that she will be compelled by your Spirit to do what is right because she understands that you are her constant companion and closest friend.

When people *are* watching, I pray she will simply do what is right out of love for you—not to be "admired by others" so that she won't "lose the reward" you have waiting for her (Matthew 6:1ᶜ).

I also ask that you will give her favor with others so that her life has an impact for you. Your Word tells us that "a good name is more desirable than great riches," and "to be esteemed is better than silver or gold" (Proverbs 22:1).

Please let her have personal integrity, Lord! "The integrity of the upright guides them" (Proverbs 11:3ᵈ). "People with integrity walk safely, but those who follow crooked paths will be exposed" (Proverbs 10:9ᵉ). Please don't let her slip and fall, Lord!

When her road is uphill, I pray she will continue to trust you to show yourself faithful.

You "personally rescued" your people again and again, and "lifted them up and carried them through all the years" (Isaiah 63:9ᶠ). May the sweetness of your Spirit give her the strength she needs to choose your ways above all others.

Our ways are in your "full view," Father (Proverbs 5:21). And one day, you "will bring to light what is hidden in darkness and will expose the motives" of our hearts (1 Corinthians 4:5).

Even "the good deeds done in secret will someday come to light" (1 Timothy 5:25[g]). When all is revealed, may her actions show she loves you most of all!

a NLT, b NLT, c NLT, d ESV, e NLT, f NLT, g NLT

Day 40

TENDING THE TEMPLE

> Do you not know that your bodies are
> temples of the Holy Spirit, who is in you,
> whom you have received from God?
> You are not your own; you were bought
> at a price. Therefore honor God with your
> bodies.
>
> 1 Corinthians 6:19–20

I pray that my child will take good care of herself, Lord. And not just for her benefit—I pray she will do it for you. May she "honor" you with her body (1 Corinthians 6:20)!

What amazing bodies you have given us!

We are truly "fearfully and wonderfully made; your works are wonderful" (Psalm 139:14)!

You are so good to take the things we need to do to stay alive—like eating and drinking—and make them pleasurable!

Every sense we may have been blessed with—taste, touch, sight, smell, hearing—is a gift from you. I pray that my child will never take one of these gifts for granted, and will thank you for every one she has.

Let her marvel at them, and use them to praise you for even the smallest blessings of flavor, sound, color, texture, or smell.

Please help her to understand how deeply you care "about our bodies" (1 Corinthians 6:13ᵃ). "Even the hairs" of her head "are all numbered" (Luke 12:7ᵇ)!

I also ask that she will comprehend that her body exists for you and is "a temple" of your Holy Spirit (1 Corinthians 6:19ᶜ).

May she exercise and eat right, not from vanity but out of gratitude and a sense of responsibility. May she take care of all you have blessed her with so she may serve you effectively.

I pray that she will have emotional maturity and self-control when it comes to her body, so that she "will not be mastered by anything" (1 Corinthians 6:12).

Please give her the wisdom to "flee from sexual immorality" because "the sexually immoral person sins against his own body" (1 Corinthians 6:18ᵈ).

Please also protect her from the pressures in our culture to look a certain way. Give her grace to understand that her body is beautiful simply because it is your creation, and she is the work of your hands.

I pray that "the excitement of youth" will not cause her "to forget" you, her Creator (Ecclesiastes 12:1ᵉ).

When she is healthy and strong, may she know that you are "enabling" her "to stand on mountain heights" (Psalm 18:33ᶠ).

When she is sick, I pray she will know you as "the LORD who heals" (Exodus 15:26ᵍ).

Whatever her condition, may she always know you!

Then, when her life on earth is done and the "last trumpet" sounds and she is "raised imperishable" in a body that will never die, we will praise you together, saying, "Thanks be to God, who gives us the victory through our Lord Jesus Christ" (1 Corinthians 15:52, 57[h])!

a NLT, b ESV, c ESV, d ESV, e NLT, f NLT, g NLT, h ESV

RESPONSIBLE

And the Lord replied, "A faithful, sensible
servant is one to whom the master can
give the responsibility of managing
his other household servants and feeding
them. If the master returns and finds that
the servant has done a good job, there
will be a reward."

Luke 12:42–43 (NLT)

Please help my child to learn what it means to be responsible, Lord Jesus.

I pray he will be someone who can be trusted, faithful to carry out even the smallest task.

If he knows how to be "faithful in little things," he will also be "faithful in large ones" (Luke 16:10[a]).

Please help him to understand that if he compromises in matters of integrity you will notice . . . even though others may not.

When you told the parable about the "faithful, sensible servant," you were talking about so much more than earthly "responsibility" (Luke 12:42[b]). This is a kingdom thing, Lord. You said that if we are "dishonest in little things," we "won't be honest with greater responsibilities." And if we are "untrustworthy about worldly wealth," we won't be able to handle "the true riches of heaven" (Luke 16:10–11[c]).

So I pray my child will always be preparing for your kingdom and will look for it to "come soon" (Luke 11:2[d])!

Whether he's cleaning his room, completing an exam, or filling out a tax return, I ask that you will help him to be honest and faithful to you. You even promised "a reward" for those who are (Luke 12:43[e])!

Please protect him from the ungodly influence of "those of this world whose reward is in this life" (Psalm 17:14). "Evil people get rich for the moment, but the reward of the godly will last" (Proverbs 11:18[f]).

Help him to remember that he is living for so much more than this world. "Each person is destined to die once and after that comes judgment" (Hebrews 9:27[g]).

You told us that "a time is coming when all who are in their graves" will hear your voice "and come out"—and "those who have done what is good will rise to live" (John 5:28–29). I want him to live forever in your kingdom and be richly rewarded!

I pray he will be among those "longing for a better country— a heavenly one." Because you are "not ashamed to be called their God," and you have "prepared a city for them" (Hebrews 11:16)!

But beyond any reward, I pray he will simply look forward to *you*. May he long for you more than anything else.

I pray my child will love you for who you are, not just for
what you can do for him. Please help him to seek your
face and not just your hand![3]

When he thinks of all that is to come and all you've promised,
I pray he will think of you most of all. You are the one
who makes it heaven!

a NLT, b NLT, c NLT, d NLT, e NLT, f NLT, g NLT

---

3.   For more on this concept as it relates to prayer, please see Daniel Henderson's
      book *Fresh Encounters*. Colorado Springs, CO: NavPress, 2004, pp. 90–91.

THAT ALL MAY GO WELL

Children, obey your parents because you
belong to the Lord, for this is the right thing
to do. "Honor your father and mother."
This is the first commandment with a promise: If you honor your father and mother,
"things will go well for you, and you will
have a long life on the earth."

Ephesians 6:1–3 (NLT)

I want my child to be as blessed as possible, Father. But for that to happen, you alone determine which blessings are best.

Sometimes when I say, 'I want the best things for her,' I'm reminded of how easy it is for me to see "things merely from a human point of view," and not from yours (Matthew 16:23[a]).

But your Word shows me the right direction. "Things will go well" for my child (Ephesians 6:3[b]) if both of us obey and honor you.

If I don't "do what is right," "love mercy," and "walk humbly" with you (Micah 6:8[c]), I will make it very difficult for her to honor or obey me.

How could I insist that she honor the dishonorable or obey the disobedient?

I pray that you will help me to live an exemplary life before her, Lord, a life that lovingly points to you.

I ask that she will see you in me, Lord Jesus, and be drawn to you, "the shepherd" of her soul (1 Peter 2:25[d]).

You know what we're up against, Lord. The "rebellion" of our world lays "heavy upon it" (Isaiah 24:20).

In a world that does not honor you, it would be easier for my child to 'go with the flow' and rebel at times. But I ask that you protect her from "the spirit who is now at work in those who are disobedient" (Ephesians 2:2), and help her "not conform to the pattern of this world" (Romans 12:2).

I pray she will be an original—your original!

I pray that she will want to "respect" her "mother and father" (Leviticus 19:3[e]) because she wants to honor and obey *you*. You promised that she will be blessed if she does that!

Help her to "show proper respect to everyone" (1 Peter 2:17). I ask that a healthy respect for authority will be a consistent part of her life.

May she "give to everyone" what they are owed; "taxes and government fees to those who collect them," and "respect and honor to those who are in authority" (Romans 13:7[f]).

But may she honor your authority most of all.

You tell us that "those who love your instructions have great peace and do not stumble" (Psalm 119:165[g]). Lord, I want that for her!

It's not about legalism, is it, Father? It's about love! Love that inspires her to live with vision and purpose for something and someone much larger than herself—you! May she always be "aware of your unfailing love" and live "according to your truth" (Psalm 26:3[h]).

a NLT, b NLT, c NLT, d ESV, e NLT, f NLT, g NLT, h NLT

Week 7

FRUITFUL

The Mess and the Message

Bestow, dear Lord, upon our youth,
The gift of saving grace;
And let the seed of sacred truth
Fall in a fruitful place.

William Cowper

God has a way of planting the most fruitful seeds where we never see them. Some of the most difficult circumstances of our lives become fertile ground for growth we never expected, and fruit that could not have come any other way.

God wastes nothing. He is even able to take what the adversary meant for evil and turn it to good, "the saving of many lives" (Genesis 50:20). Nowhere did this become more apparent in my own life than in our son's struggle with substance abuse.

Our son went through a heartbreaking season that lasted seven years. God would eventually set him free from a severe addiction and is using him powerfully today in a ministry that helps others who wrestle in similar ways. He has a unique, hard-won ability to understand what addicts are going through and to share the difference Jesus has made in his life in a winsome, non-judgmental way. When I asked my son if he minded if I shared the change God had made in his life, his response was, "Dad, I want you to tell it. I *prefer* that you tell my story, because it's pointless if others don't hear about it. Why else would God have done it?"

Baseball great Darryl Strawberry shares that perspective. After earning eight all-star selections and four World Series rings, his brilliant seventeen-year career was ruined by addiction. But then Jesus saved him and set him free. Since he met the Lord, Strawberry has dedicated his life to ministering to other athletes caught in the web he once knew. He summed up God's transformation of his life with these words: "Here I am, a baseball superstar, falling into the pits, having everybody write you off and then having God say, 'I'm going to use your mess for a message.' How beautiful is that?"[4]

When God's Spirit is at work, beautiful fruit can grow from the same ground where before there was only decay. This week we are boldly praying for the fruit of the Spirit in our children's lives: "love, joy, peace, patience, kindness, goodness, faithfulness, gentleness, and self-control" (Galatians 5:22–23 NLT).

God deeply desires to bring all of these things into our children's hearts as they live in him. Pray with faith! He is able to use our prayers to plant seeds even where there's a mess. And the message that grows out of that ground will be to His glory.

---

4. Bob Nightengale, "Pastor Strawberry Says True Calling Ahead, Not Baseball," *USA Today*, July 12, 2013.

Day 43

"I LOVE YOU, DADDY"

The fruit of the Spirit is love. . . .
I love you, O Lord, my strength.

Galatians 5:22, Psalm 18:1 (ESV)

I love to hear my child say 'I love you.'

I love *you*, Lord, and praise you for the blessing of being a parent.

Having a child teaches me so much about your heart and how much you love us.

It shows me the incredible depth of your sacrifice, Father. You did not "spare" your "own Son but gave him up for us all" (Romans 8:32[a]) because you love us so much!

I cannot imagine the pain you went through on our behalf.

Lord Jesus, I praise you that your life-giving sacrifice for us on the cross is "accomplished" (Luke 12:50[b]), and that you now have gone "to the Father" and have "loved" your own "to the end" (John 13:1). You will "reign forever and ever" (Revelation 11:15[c])!

How can we not love you for all you have done for us?

"We know that we live" in you and you live in us, because you have also "given us" your "Spirit" (1 John 4:13)!

We "have not received a spirit that makes" us "fearful slaves." Instead, we "received" your Spirit when you "adopted" us as your "own children." And "now we" can even "call" you, "Abba, Father" (Romans 8:15[d])—another way of saying 'Daddy!'

Abba, I pray my child will give you the joy of her saying, 'I love you, Daddy,' not only with words, but through a life lived intentionally for you.

I pray that my child will "love" you with all her "heart," "soul," and "mind" (Matthew 22:37[e]).

May she love you through and through, living each day expectantly in your presence, recognizing all she is and has belongs to you.

Because of your tender "mercies" to her, I pray she will "present" herself to you "as a living sacrifice, holy and acceptable" to you. May she understand that honoring you with her body is also "spiritual worship" (Romans 12:1[f]).

I pray that her life will bring forth love that is the beautiful "fruit of the Spirit" (Galatians 5:22) of all who sincerely follow you.

May she love you more than self—more even than life—understanding that you, "along with" Jesus, will "graciously give us all things" (Romans 8:32)!

"What shall we say" about the "wonderful things" you have done for us and will continue to do? If you are for us, "who can ever be against us?" (Romans 8:31[g]).

"I love you, O LORD, my strength" (Psalm 18:1[h]). And I pray my child will love you too!

a ESV, b ESV, c NLT, d NLT, e ESV, f ESV, g NLT, h ESV

Day 44

STRONG IN JOY

But the fruit of the Spirit is . . . joy . . . .
"Don't be dejected and sad, for the joy of
the Lord is your strength!"

Galatians 5:22,
Nehemiah 8:10 (NLT)

Thank you for the joy you give, Father.

There's nothing like it! Your joy is alive; it is the result of your "Spirit living within" us (Romans 8:11[a])!

Your Word tells us that just as you "raised Christ Jesus from the dead," you "will give life" even to our "mortal bodies" (Romans 8:11[b]) because your Spirit is alive in us.

"How precious to me are your thoughts, O God!" (Psalm 139:17).

You save us and make us new, giving us life from the inside out!

You are joy, Lord Jesus! How can we ever have a deep and lasting happiness apart from you?

I pray my child will know the joy you give because he genuinely knows *you*.

May he have a close and tender relationship with you that gives him daily access to inexhaustible joy—joy that is more than a feeling, joy that is the outcome of sincerely following you!

I pray he will take the steps that he needs to walk into your joy every day.

I pray my child will learn to praise you even when he doesn't feel like it, Lord. I'm reminded of the time Nehemiah told the people of Israel to choose joy. He instructed them not to "be dejected and sad," because your "joy" was their "strength" (Nehemiah 8:10ᶜ).

When David was going through one of the most difficult times in his life he told you, "My heart is confident in you, O God; my heart is confident. No wonder I can sing your praises! Wake up, my heart!" (Psalm 57:7–8ᵈ).

I ask that you awaken my son's heart to the wonder of all that you are!

I pray that he will discipline himself to praise you, just like David did. He said, "I *will* praise you, LORD, with all my heart; I *will* tell of all the marvelous things you have done. I *will* be filled with joy because of you. I *will* sing praises to your name, O Most High" (Psalm 9:1–2ᵉ).

No human being can fully contain the joy you give. I pray your joy will overflow from my son's heart into the lives of others. May your "joy" be in him so his "joy may be complete" (John 15:11)!

Please give him the wisdom to stay away from the sadness of sin and its "fleeting pleasures" (Hebrews 11:25ᶠ).

You alone can give us true bliss. Only "you will show" him "the way of life," granting him "the joy of your presence and the pleasures of living with you forever" (Psalm 16:11^g).

May the fruit of your joy grow and mature in my child's life, Lord Jesus. May he be an example of true happiness in you!

PERFECT PEACE

> But the fruit of the Spirit is . . . peace . . . .
> You will keep in perfect peace all who
> trust in you, all whose thoughts are fixed
> on you!
>
> Galatians 5:22, Isaiah 26:3 (NLT)

I praise you for your peace, Lord Jesus.

You are the "Prince of Peace" (Isaiah 9:6[a]), and you promise "peace" to your "people" (Psalm 85:8).

You told us, "I am leaving you with a gift—peace of mind and heart. And the peace I give is a gift the world cannot give. So don't be troubled or afraid" (John 14:27[b]).

I pray that my child will live with your peace in her heart, Lord.

I know that can only happen if she walks with you every day, for that path is where "happiness is found" (Psalm 119:35[c]).

Please give her grace to understand that her salvation is found in "repentance and rest" in you (Isaiah 30:15), and that you will give her fresh strength as she quietly trusts in you.

Please help her to rest in your wisdom for her life, so she may understand that your ways are "pleasant ways," and all of your "paths are peace" (Proverbs 3:17). "A heart at peace" even "gives life to the body" (Proverbs 14:30)!

May she have wisdom beyond her years to see through the world's counterfeit comforts and to comprehend that "there is no peace" apart from you (Isaiah 48:22).

I ask that you bless my child with friends who will set an example of what it's like to live in your peace. May she "look at those who are honest and good" and learn from them, because "a wonderful future awaits those who love peace" (Psalm 37:37[d]).

I pray that she will love peace! May she love being near you, and have a hunger for your peace that keeps her coming back to your Word and to worship and prayer.

May she understand that your peace for her was hard won, Lord Jesus, and that we only "have peace with God" (Romans 5:1) through your "blood, shed on the cross" (Colossians 1:20).

Because of this, may she "make every effort to be found spotless, blameless and at peace" with you (2 Peter 3:14), and to live "a life of goodness and peace and joy" in the strength that comes through your Holy Spirit (Romans 14:17[e]).

May your peace "rule" in her heart! (Colossians 3:15[f]).

I ask that you, "the Lord of peace" will give my child "peace at all times and in every way" (2 Thessalonians 3:16).

I pray that you, "the God of peace," will "sanctify" her "through and through." May her "whole spirit, soul and body be kept blameless" at the day of your return, Lord Jesus. I praise you because you are "faithful" and you will "do it" (1 Thessalonians 5:23–24)!

Day 46

BEST REST

But the fruit of the Spirit is . . . patience. . . .
We also pray that you will be strengthened with all his glorious power
so you will have all the endurance and
patience you need.
May you be filled with joy.

Galatians 5:22 (NLT),
Colossians 1:11 (NLT)

I pray that you will teach my child the secret of patience, Lord.

Please help him to understand that patience is found by resting in you.

We always need patience when we are waiting for something; may he wait for *you* most of all!

I pray that the cry of his heart will be, "I wait for the LORD, my soul waits, and in his word I put my hope" (Psalm 130:5).

If his heart is set on you, everything else will be placed in perspective. He can face life with a thankful heart knowing "all things" are his already (1 Corinthians 3:21[a]), because you have "enabled" him "to share in the inheritance" that belongs to your "people, who live in the light" (Colossians 1:12[b]).

I pray my child "will be strengthened" with all the "glorious power" you give, so that he "will have all the endurance and patience" he needs (Colossians 1:11[c]).

Holy Spirit, I ask that you fill him with your loving presence, so that he will be "be joyful in hope, patient in affliction," and "faithful in prayer" (Romans 12:12).

I pray that whenever he has to wait, he will learn to fill the moments by turning to you in prayer.

Our world wants everything 'yesterday' and conditions us to demand our own way. But your Word tells us, "Wait for the LORD and keep *his* way, and he will exalt you" (Psalm 37:34[d]).

I pray that he will "be strong and take heart and wait" for you (Psalm 27:14), looking for your will and way above his own.

When things happen that try his patience, please help him to learn simple contentment in your presence, enjoying your company.

Give him the grace to say with David, "I have calmed and quieted my soul" (Psalm 131:2[e]), and to place his hope in you.

No matter how badly he wants something, may he quiet himself with this thought: "Return to your rest, my soul, for the LORD has been good to you" (Psalm 116:7).

"Whoever is patient has great understanding" (Proverbs 14:29), and "knowledge of" you, "the Holy One, *is* understanding" (Proverbs 9:10, italics added).

"Better to be patient than powerful; better to have self-control than to conquer a city" (Proverbs 16:32[f]).

May his strength be in you! Please help him to walk with you in "all humility and gentleness, with patience, bearing with" others "in love" (Ephesians 4:2[g]).

You have such beautiful patience with us, Lord, and I pray my child will learn from you. May he stay so close to your heart that your patience shines through him!

a ESV, b NLT, c NLT, d ESV *italics added*, e ESV, f NLT, g ESV

GRACE-FULL

But the fruit of the Spirit is . . . kindness,
goodness . . .
And God is able to make all grace
abound to you, so that having all suf-
ficiency in all things at all times, you may
abound in every good work.

Galatians 5:22,
2 Corinthians 9:8 (ESV)

I praise you for your grace to us, Father.

When we were "dead" in our "transgressions and sins" (Ephesians 2:1) you showed incredible "kindness to us in Christ Jesus" (Ephesians 2:7).

You "canceled the record of the charges against us and took it away by nailing it to the cross" (Colossians 2:14ᵃ).

In your "great mercy" you even gave "us new birth into a living hope through the resurrection of Jesus Christ from the dead" (1 Peter 1:3).

You "forgave us all our sins" and made us "alive with Christ" (Colossians 2:13)—and you didn't have to do it!

But you did it because you are so good. You held nothing back from us, not even your only Son!

You keep on giving to us in every way. You even "make all grace abound" to us, so that "in all things at all times," we may "abound in every good work" (2 Corinthians 9:8).

I pray that my child may have "life by the power" of your name (John 20:31[b]), a relationship "filled with the fruit of righteousness that comes through" you "to the glory and praise of God" (Philippians 1:11)!

"Your compassion, LORD, is great" (Psalm 119:156), and I ask that she will be filled with it!

May your love shine from her soul because she is filled with your Spirit. Where your Spirit is, "there is freedom" (2 Corinthians 3:17[c]). Freedom to grow in the hope that lives and breathes within us, and boldness to share the wonder of who you are with others.

I pray that my child will bear as "much fruit" (John 15:8[d]) for you as she possibly can, Lord Jesus. May your "kindness" and "goodness" (Galatians 5:22) be one of the first things others see in her!

"You, LORD, are good" (Psalm 25:7), and you "will never stop doing good" for your people (Jeremiah 32:40)!

You are so kind to us, and I pray my child will "continue to trust" in your "kindness" (Romans 11:22[e]) day after day. May your kindness be her continual inspiration for having compassion for others.

One day, you "will give eternal life to those who keep on doing good" (Romans 2:6–7[f]). I ask that she will never "get tired of doing what is good," so that she may "reap a harvest of blessing" (Galatians 6:9[g])!

a NLT, b NLT, c ESV, d ESV, e NLT, f NLT, g NLT

CROWNED WITH FAITHFULNESS

But the fruit of the Spirit is . . .
faithfulness . . . "Where you go I will go,
and where you stay I will stay.
Your people will be my people and your
God my God."

Galatians 5:22, Ruth 1:16

You blessed Ruth for her faithfulness in a beautiful way, Father.

When she promised to stay with Naomi instead of choosing an easier life, you took care of her and provided for all her needs.

When Ruth told Naomi, "Your God will be my God" (Ruth 1:16[a]) even though she was from Moab and not from Israel, you became her God and gave her "a future hope" (Proverbs 23:18).

You not only blessed her during her lifetime—you blessed her beyond it, for generations to come! Matthew records her name in the lineage of kings, including David and

Solomon and even Jesus (see Matthew 1:1–16). How you must love faithfulness, Lord!

You are "a faithful God who does no wrong" (Deuteronomy 32:4).

How faithful you are to receive us! When we were "living apart from Christ," we were "excluded" from your people and "without hope" (Ephesians 2:12[b]). But now we "can come" to you "through the same Holy Spirit because of what Christ has done for us (Ephesians 2:18[c]).

I pray that my child will grow in the faithfulness that your Spirit gives so freely to those who come to you.

May he learn faithfulness from you, "the faithful Holy One" (Hosea 11:12)!

"To the faithful you show yourself faithful," and "to those with integrity you show integrity" (2 Samuel 22:26[d]).

I pray that he "will search for faithful people" to be his "companions" (Psalm 101:6[e]), and to enjoy the company of those who love and know you.

I ask that you will give him strength to be faithful whether times are good or difficult, because you "will not forsake" your "faithful ones" (Psalm 37:28).

I pray that he will go to you with "ears wide open" and "listen" to "find life." Then he will know "all the unfailing love" you have "promised to David" (Isaiah 55:3[f]), all of his life and beyond!

If he is a "faithful and wise servant," then he will be "blessed" on the day you return (Matthew 24:45–46[g]).

Please give him grace so that he will "always want to obey you," and inspire in him a "love for you" that "never changes" (1 Chronicles 29:18[h]).

You "are faithful in all" you do (Psalm 33:4), Lord. Please make my child brave and strong and true!

Then he will "remain faithful even when facing death," and you who are always faithful "will give" him "the crown of life" (Revelation 2:10[i])!

a NLT, b NLT, c NLT, d NLT, e NLT, f NLT, g ESV, h NLT, i NLT

APPLES, STICKS, AND STONES

> But the fruit of the Spirit is . . . gentleness
> and self-control . . . .
> A word fitly spoken is like apples of gold in
> a setting of silver.
>
> Galatians 5:22–23,
> Proverbs 25:11 (ESV)

Words are such powerful things, Lord.

Sometimes we treat them so casually. Even when we're little we say that 'sticks and stones will break my bones, but words will never hurt me.'

But words *do* hurt! They break hearts and homes and sometimes we carry those words with us for years.

Yet words can also do good! "A word fitly spoken" is a beautiful thing, "like apples of gold in a setting of silver" (Proverbs 25:11[a]).

Your Word tells us that "the tongue has the power of life and death, and those who love it will eat its fruit" (Proverbs 18:21).

So today I pray that the words my child speaks will bear good fruit, fruit that brings life and health to others.

Please give her wisdom when it comes to words, Lord. "Wise words satisfy like a good meal; the right words bring satisfaction" (Proverbs 18:20[b]).

I pray that her words will be satisfying because they will be filled with your love and your Spirit.

May she have a way with words, Lord Jesus. *Your* way! I pray that the fruit of your Spirit in "gentleness and self-control" (Galatians 5:23) will be especially evident in the way she uses words.

I ask that you will help her to watch her words closely. You have told us that, "on the day of judgment," we will "give account for every careless word" we have spoken (Matthew 12:36–37[c]).

How we need your help in this! "We all make many mistakes." If we could really learn to control our tongues, we "could also control ourselves in every other way" (James 3:2[d]).

How many times have we wished we could pull words back as soon as they came out of our mouths? I pray that you will help my child to be "quick to listen, slow to speak, and slow to become angry" (James 1:19).

I ask that you will help her to choose her words carefully when emotions run hot, because "a gentle answer deflects anger, but harsh words make tempers flare" (Proverbs 15:1[e]).

Please also give her the wisdom to understand that gossip is a hurtful sin. "A troublemaker plants seeds of strife; gossip separates the best of friends" (Proverbs 16:28[f]). "The words of the wicked are like a murderous ambush, but the words of the godly save lives" (Proverbs 12:6[g]).

Be in her words, Lord Jesus! I pray they will point to you with power and love.

You not only save lives, you save souls! May the words she uses "be good and helpful," and "encouragement to those who hear them" (Ephesians 4:29[h]).

May "the message" about you, "in all its richness," fill her life (Colossians 3:16[i])!

a ESV, b NLT, c ESV, d NLT, e NLT, f NLT, g NLT, h NLT, i NLT

Week 8

THANKFUL

More Yours Than Mine

> I would maintain that thanks are the highest form of thought, and that gratitude is happiness doubled by wonder.
>
> G. K. Chesterton

Her name meant "favored by God," but she didn't always feel that way.

Hannah had prayed and prayed for God to give her a child. One day she pleaded with God so passionately that when Eli the priest overheard her, "he thought she had been drinking" (1 Samuel 1:13 NLT).

Not long afterward, Hannah's prayers were answered. She gave the baby a name that would perpetually remind her and others how God had answered her prayer. She named him *Samuel,* which means "heard by God" (see 1 Samuel 1:20).

But a name wasn't enough. Hanna was just getting started. When Samuel was a little older she brought him back to Eli. "Sir, do you remember me?" Hannah asked. "I am the woman who stood here several years ago praying to the Lord. I asked the Lord to give me this boy, and he has granted my request. Now I am giving him to the Lord, and he will belong to the Lord his whole life" (1 Samuel 1:25–28 NLT).

Samuel was a gift from God, and Hannah knew it. She was so thankful that she *gave him up* to God, doing her best to help Samuel know, love, and serve the Lord as long as he lived.

He would become one of the greatest prophets and leaders in Israel's history.

Hannah didn't just *say* "thank you" to God. She *lived* her thankfulness. An entire nation would be blessed for generations as a result. And it all started with a passionate prayer.

God's best blessings come into our children's lives when we energetically pray for them. This week we're thanking God for our children as well as praying for thankfulness in their hearts. You'll find prayers here about practical matters like attitudes, accepting our bodies the way God made them, strength and joy in the face of fear, enjoying God's creation, living with compassion for others, and more.

I hope you'll remember Hannah as you pray. She was so thankful for her child that she gave him up to God. She accepted the truth that her child belonged to Him even more than he did to her, and she passionately prayed for God's will to be done in his life.

Shouldn't we do the same?

GRATITUDE ATTITUDE

Give thanks in all circumstances,
for this is God's will for you in Christ Jesus.
1 Thessalonians 5:18

The first time I saw her I was so thankful, Father.

Ten tiny fingers. Ten pink and perfect toes. A tender, priceless gift from your heart and hand.

I was grateful then, and I still am! How could I not be? How blessed I am to have a child!

I pray that you will always help us to be thankful for the little things, Lord. Isn't that one of the secrets to a happy life?

Everything starts with you. Every gift. Every moment. Every breath. You are "the Creator" and "are worthy of eternal praise" (Romans 1:25[a]).

I praise you for the gift of life, Lord! And I praise you even more for the privilege of knowing you.

I pray that you will help both me and my child to take to heart the importance of being "thankful in all circumstances." I know this is what you want us to do—this is your "will" for us! (1 Thessalonians 5:18[b]).

If she is able to keep her eyes on you she will always have something to be thankful for, even when life is difficult.

This is your example for us, Lord Jesus. Even the night before you suffered so much for us—when you were wrongfully arrested, beaten and crucified—you "gave thanks to God" (1 Corinthians 11:24ᶜ).

What amazing love for the Father, Jesus, and for us! And what faith!

Your beautiful relationship with the Father and your ability to keep your eyes on what mattered most shows us what our lives should be like.

Please help us to have the same kind of thankfulness, Jesus, and to "press on to know" you (Hosea 6:3ᵈ)!

You gave yourself for us so that we "should no longer live" for ourselves, but for you "who died for" us and were "raised again" (2 Corinthians 5:15).

Please fill us with your Spirit and your love in such a way that fresh thankfulness overflows into every part of our lives.

May we make "every thought captive" to you (2 Corinthians 10:5ᵉ) so that we live for your purposes above all—and learn to thank you with new awareness for even the slightest taste, touch, sight or sound.

And when we find it challenging to be grateful because of circumstances, please give us grace in the moment to thank you by faith, so that we "continually offer" to you "a sacrifice of praise—the fruit of lips that openly profess" your name (Hebrews 13:15).

"Whatever" we do, "whether in word or deed," may we "do it all in" your name, loving you, living for you, and "giving thanks to God the Father" through you (Colossians 3:17).

May we never forget how blessed we are because of you!

a NLT, b NLT, c NLT, d NLT, e ESV

HEART MUSIC

Speaking to one another with psalms,
hymns, and songs from the Spirit.
Sing and make music from your heart to
the Lord, always giving thanks to God the
Father for everything, in the name of our
Lord Jesus Christ.

Ephesians 5:19–20

I love to hear my child sing, Lord.

It doesn't even matter if he hits the right notes—it's just good to hear his voice.

Something tells me that you feel the same way. You made us to sing, and your Word teaches us in so many places . . .

"Sing praises to God, sing praises; sing praises to our King, sing praises" (Psalm 47:6)!

"Is anyone happy? Let them sing songs of praise" (James 5:13).

"Let all who take refuge in you be glad; let them ever sing for joy" (Psalm 5:11).

I pray that my child will always want to "sing and make music" (Ephesians 5:19) in his heart to you, Lord Jesus.

We sing when we're happy, and I pray he will be happy in you!

May he have the happiness that springs from a thankful soul, because he has a living relationship with you that will never end.

May he know he is a child of the king! Then he will "be grateful for receiving a kingdom that cannot be shaken" (Hebrews 12:28[a]) and want to worship you for it!

I pray my son will say from the heart, "I will sing the Lord's praise, for he has been good to me" (Psalm 13:6).

I ask also that your songs will fill his mind instead of the world's music. Sometimes songs get stuck in our heads and bring the same thought to mind again and again. So I pray his thoughts will be filled with you!

May he praise you through the day and even sing "songs in the night" (Psalm 77:6) because he lives without fear and knows that "even the darkness will not be dark to you," for "darkness is as light to you" (Psalm 139:12).

I pray he will rest securely in you and "sing for joy in the shadow of your wings" (Psalm 63:7[b]).

What could be better than knowing you will always watch over us?

"You guide" us "with your counsel, and afterward you will take" us "into glory" (Psalm 73:24).

But until then, we keep growing stronger because of your grace! We "go from strength to strength" (Psalm 84:7) when we set our hearts on seeking you.

May his life be a symphony of praise to you, Lord—a masterpiece of melodies from the heart—a joy for you to hear!

May he say, "I will sing to the LORD as long as I live. I will praise my God to my last breath!" (Psalm 104:33ᶜ).

Then, when his life on this earth is done, the music will only grow sweeter. He will join with "every creature in heaven and on earth and under the earth and on the sea, and all that is in them," singing, "To him who sits on the throne and to the Lamb be praise and honor and glory and power, for ever and ever!" (Revelation 5:13).

a ESV, b NLT, c NLT

OVER WHAT'S UNDER THE BED

Let them praise his name with dancing
and make music to him
with timbrel and harp. For the LORD takes
delight in his people;
he crowns the humble with victory. Let his
faithful people rejoice
in this honor and sing for joy on their beds.

Psalm 149:3–5

Sometimes our children want us to leave the nightlight on . . . and close the closet door . . . and check under the bed.

Nighttime isn't always easy, Lord. It's hard to go to sleep when imaginations run wild.

So today I pray that you will calm my child's fears and give her your peace. I ask that you chase her fears away so she may awaken to a bright new morning in your love. "Joy *comes* in the morning" (Psalm 30:5ᵃ)!

I ask that she will not only rest in you; I pray that she will "rejoice" in you (Philippians 3:1ᵇ), even if that means "dancing" and that she will "sing for joy" (Psalm 149:3, 5) on her bed!

May she have not just an occasional smile or a hopeful thought, but real joy in you.

You once told your people, "you will go free, leaping with joy like calves let out to pasture" (Malachi 4:2ᶜ).

May my child know the joy David did, and say with him, "The LORD is my strength and my shield; my heart trusts in him, and he helps me. My heart leaps for joy, and with my song I praise him" (Psalm 28:7).

May your joy 'jump' within her as she understands how blessed she is to be saved and to belong to you. I pray she will have a thankful heart!

There's no joy like the joy you give. May it be her prized possession, something she treasures as long as she lives.

But I also ask that it will be something she gives away. I pray that she will let her "light shine before others, so that they may see" (Matthew 5:16ᵈ) the good things she does for you and praise you for them.

May she live for "the praise" of your "glory" (Ephesians 1:12), enthusiastic in your love, pointing others to you!

No matter how many years she sees, I pray she will always "receive the kingdom of God like a child" (Mark 10:15ᵉ), with a fresh, open-eyed faith that looks forward to each new day.

But I also ask that you bless her with an 'even though' faith: "Even though the fig trees have no blossoms, and there are no grapes on the vines; even though the olive crop fails, and the fields lie empty and barren; even though the flocks die in the fields, and the cattle barns are empty, yet I will rejoice in the LORD! I will be joyful in the God of my salvation!" (Habakkuk 3:17–18ᶠ)

Please bless her with a faith that stays steady through the ups and downs of life, because you are Lord over all of it!

May she always be thankful for you, Father. You promise in your Word, "My servants will sing out of the joy of their hearts" (Isaiah 65:14).

May her heart sing and dance in the joy of your presence today, tomorrow, and forever!

a NKJV, b ESV, c NLT, d ESV, e ESV, f NLT

VIRTUOUS REALITY

O Lord, what a variety of things you have
made!
In wisdom you have made them all. The
earth is full of
your creatures . . . May the glory of the
Lord continue forever!
The Lord takes pleasure in all he has
made!

Psalm 104:24, 31 (NLT)

Sometimes the beauty of what you have made takes my breath away, Lord.

The majesty of a midnight sky, the intricacy of a baby's hand, the sunsets you paint day after day . . . So many masterpieces, each one unique!

I can see why you "looked over all" you had made and "saw that it was very good!" (Genesis 1:31ᵃ).

How amazing you are, Lord! You just spoke it into existence, and there it was! All of creation . . . sun, moon, and stars, worlds beyond counting.

I pray that my child will never lose her sense of wonder at what you have created, no matter how many years she is blessed with. May she be captivated by "the work of your hands" (Hebrews 1:10) and grateful to you for it.

I pray she will spend time outside enjoying what you have made, preferring your brilliance to the dull flicker and 'virtual reality' of a man-made screen.

"The heavens proclaim" your "glory" and "the skies display" your "craftsmanship." "Day after day they continue to speak; night after night they make" you "known" (Psalm 19:1–2[b])!

As she takes in the beauty of the world around her, I pray she will sense the symphony of your creative genius and power.

"All things were made through" you (John 1:3[c])! Though science can help us understand how things happen, it can only tell part of the story. Speak to her spirit, Lord. Give her a glimpse behind the details at the artistry beyond.

We were "created for" your "glory," "formed and made" (Isaiah 43:7) so we may know and praise you along with "all your works" (Psalm 145:10[d]).

Your Word tells us that "the creation looks forward to the day when it will join" your children "in glorious freedom from death and decay" (Romans 8:21[e]). It says, "Let the rivers clap their hands; let the hills sing for joy together" (Psalm 98:8[f]). "Let the fields and their crops burst out with joy! Let the trees of the forest rustle with praise" before you, for you are "coming!" (Psalm 96:12–13[g]).

You are coming to take all that is wrong and set it right. One day, you will create "a new heaven and a new earth" (Revelation 21:1[h]).

If there is so much beauty in the world as it is now, I can only imagine what it will be like then! Not a hint of sin or death . . . the 'virtuous reality' you intended before the dawn of "the first day" (Genesis 1:5[i]).

I pray my child will "look forward" to the day of your return and "speed its coming," Lord Jesus (2 Peter 3:12), so she may live an undying life in the goodness of your presence forever!

a NLT, b NLT, c ESV, d ESV, e NLT, f ESV, g NLT, h ESV, i ESV

COMPASSION'S REWARD

"And if you give even a cup of cold water
to one of the least of my followers, you will
surely be rewarded."

Matthew 10:42 (NLT)

Your Word tells of so many times when you "had compassion" for others (Matthew 9:36ᵃ), Lord Jesus . . .

. . . when you "saw a large crowd" and then "healed their sick" (Matthew 14:14).

. . . when you encountered "two blind men" who "were sitting by the roadside" (Matthew 20:30).

. . . when "a man with leprosy" came to you and "begged" before you "on his knees" (Mark 1:40).

Each time you served them and helped them and loved them!

You are "full of compassion and mercy" (James 5:11)! And I pray that my child will "have the same attitude" (Philippians 2:5ᵇ).

Please give him a compassionate heart like yours, Lord Jesus!

Give him grace so that he won't "look out" only for his "own interests." May he "take an interest in others, too" (Philippians 2:4[c]).

I pray that his compassion will flow from a thankful heart because his life has been filled with your "great love" and he knows "the wonderful things" you have done for him (Psalm 107:15[d]).

You promised that he will "be rewarded" for even the little things like giving "a cup of cold water" (Matthew 10:42[e]), so I ask that he will show kindness in ways both large and small.

When he goes through struggles and challenges, I pray you will use those moments to help him feel deeply for others who wrestle in the same ways.

May he discover the truth that you comfort us "in all our troubles, so that we can comfort those in any trouble with the comfort we ourselves receive" from you (2 Corinthians 1:4).

Your Word teaches that "pure and genuine religion in the sight of God the Father means caring for orphans and widows in their distress and refusing to let the world corrupt" us (James 1:27[f]).

Please keep him from the world's selfish ways, Lord, and give him grace to look after those who have less than he.

Help him not to focus on what he does not have; help him instead to see all he does have because of the simple fact that he belongs to you.

I ask that he will learn to "do good to everyone—especially to those in the family of faith" (Galatians 6:10[g]).

Because you served us so humbly, Lord Jesus, the Father lifted you "to the place of highest honor" and gave you "the name above all other names" (Philippians 2:9[h]).

I pray my child will be rewarded too, Lord. May you be the "one thing" he seeks (Psalm 27:4) most of all!

May your love grow "more perfect" in him as he lives "like" you "here in this world" (1 John 4:17[i]).

a ESV, b NLT, c NLT, d NLT, e NLT, f NLT, g NLT, h NLT, i NLT

RISE AND SHINE!

For we are God's masterpiece.
He has created us anew in Christ Jesus,
so we can do the good things he planned
for us long ago.

Ephesians 2:10 (NLT)

I pray that my child will be thankful for the way you made her, Father.

You made her a "masterpiece" (Ephesians 2:10[a])!

You "formed" her in her "mother's womb" (Ecclesiastes 11:5), weaving each strand of DNA into a one-of-a-kind creation. There has never been anyone like her, and there will never be another!

I pray that she will rest content in the truth that she doesn't need to be anyone other than the original you made her to be.

So many people spend their lives wanting to be someone else, chasing after others who are following "their pride" (Zephaniah 3:11[b]), living for themselves and the trends of this world.

I pray she will follow you instead, and want to be what you made her to be.

You made her to know you and love you and "have life" through your Son (1 John 5:12ᶜ), a full new life brimming with purpose!

You have such "good things" (Ephesians 2:10ᵈ) planned for her! I pray she will embrace your ideas for her life and live with anticipation, looking forward to each new day with you.

No one is as creative as you, Lord! "Who can know" your "thoughts?" (Romans 11:34ᵉ). "Everything comes from" you "and exists by" your "power and is intended for" your "glory" (Romans 11:36ᶠ).

I pray she will want to live for your glory too!

Please give her grace to understand that there can be no beauty in this world apart from you. You are the source of all that "is good" (Psalm 85:12ᵍ).

I remember when my child was born—how thrilled I was to see the wonder of your work. She was precious and beautiful, just the way you made her.

The more she walks with you the more beautiful she will become, filled with "the radiance" of your light that shines from the inside when your Son lives in us (Hebrews 1:3).

"You are the fountain of life, the light by which we see!" (Psalm 36:9ʰ).

I pray she will "arise" with the fresh new life you give and "shine for all to see" as "the glory" of who you are "rises to shine" (Isaiah 60:1ⁱ) upon her soul.

May she "display" your "glory" (2 Corinthians 3:18[j]) and your beauty as you "work out" your "plans" for her life" (Psalm 138:8[k]).

May she rise to praise you each new day, deeply thankful that through "Jesus there is forgiveness" for our sins (Acts 13:38[l]).

I ask that she may "know the greatness" of all that you are (Psalm 135:5[m]), and live for nothing less than to love and serve you for all eternity!

.

DO IT AGAIN!

Lord, I have heard of your fame; I stand in
awe of your deeds, Lord.
Repeat them in our day, in our time make
them known.

Habakkuk 3:2

I'm amazed when I think about the things you've done, Lord.

You fed "five thousand men" and even more "women and children" (Matthew 14:21ᵃ) with "only five loaves of bread and two fish" (Matthew 14:17).

You walked "on the water" (John 6:19) and calmed "the wind and the sea" (Mark 4:41ᵇ) by simply speaking to them.

You made "the blind see" and "the lame walk." You cured "the lepers" and made "the deaf hear." You even raised "the dead" to "life" (Matthew 11:5ᶜ)!

And you still continue to "stretch out your hand to heal and perform miraculous signs and wonders" through your powerful "name" (Acts 4:30)!

I praise and thank you for all you do! And I pray my child will see your hand move too! I long for him to see "your works and meditate on all your mighty deeds" (Psalm 77:12).

"I stand in awe of your deeds," and ask that you "repeat them" in his day and "make them known" in his time (Habakkuk 3:2).

"Summon your power, God," and "show us your strength . . . as you have done before" (Psalm 68:28).

I pray that he will see you do even more wonderful things than I have, and thank and praise you for them! I ask that this will happen because he has faith in you, Jesus.

I'm reminded that there was a place where you "did not do many miracles" because of "their lack of faith" (Matthew 13:58). Don't let him 'live there,' Lord!

Please help him to have a deep and lasting faith in you—then he will see what only you can do!

But I also ask that his faith won't depend on personal experience and outward circumstances; then he would "never believe" in you unless he sees "miraculous signs and wonders" (John 4:48[d]).

As I pray for his faith I'm reminded of the man who came to ask your help for his child. He told you, "I do believe; help me overcome my unbelief!" (Mark 9:24).

Please help me to "set an example" for him "in conduct, in love, in faith, in purity" (1 Timothy 4:12[e]). But while I grow in these ways, I also pray that you will help me to have the faith of a child, Lord.

Little children love to say 'Do it again!' when grown-ups do something they love. And I think about the wonderful things you've done and I pray, 'Do it again!'

Do it again in my child's life, Lord! Let him see you do incredible things!

I long for him to have a faith that surpasses my own so that he will see you do even more!

You "alone" do "great wonders," Lord, and your faithful "love endures forever" (Psalm 136:4).

I thank you for the way you've shown yourself faithful in my life—and I praise you in advance for what my child will see when you 'do it again!'

a ESV, b ESV, c NLT, d NLT, e ESV

Week 9

HUMBLE

Me Third

> We must view humility as one of the
> essential things that characterizes true
> Christianity.
>
> Jonathan Edwards

If we want our children to really know and be like Jesus, we'll pray for them to be humble.

When we think of "must have" character traits for our children, humility may not be one of the first things that come to mind. But it should be, if we really want them to be blessed.

God loves to bless humble people. The Bible emphasizes this again and again:

"God opposes the proud but shows favor to the humble" (1 Peter 5:5). "He guides the humble in what is right and teaches them his way" (Psalm 25:9), and "crowns the humble with victory" (Psalm 149:4).

While God's Word tells us to be "completely humble" (Ephesians 4:2), that isn't the world's way. Living with humility requires a special kind of strength in our "me first" world. It takes strength to admit when you're wrong, to say that you're sorry, or to share the credit when you've done most of the work. When the world tells us to "be some-body," God says we will be happier if we take our eyes off ourselves and work on serving Him and others. Being hum-ble comes with a price to our pride, but it also comes with a promise: "Humble yourselves before the Lord, and he will lift you up" (James 4:10).

If we want our children to know the real height and depth of God's love, we'll ask God to help them have hum-ble hearts. Jesus was "gentle and humble in heart" and prom-ised that if we "learn" from him, we will "find rest" for our "souls" (Matthew 11:29). He set "an example" (John 13:15) for us and can be trusted to deliver on what he promises.

"Though he was God, he did not think of equality with God as something to cling to. Instead, he gave up his divine privileges"—and because He did, "God elevated him to the place of highest honor and gave him the name above all other names" (Philippians 2:6–7, 9 NLT).

Asking God to help our children be humble challenges us to be humble ourselves. We have to trust God with our most prized possessions. Praying this way isn't always easy, but as Ruth Bell Graham pointed out, "The Christian par-ent's authority will be a direct result of, and in proportion to, his or her submission to divine authority."[5] If we want to make a vital and lasting impact on our children, we'll ask for what matters most to God.

---

5. Graham, *Prodigals and Those Who Love Them*, p. 75.

An old Puritan prayer pleads, "Let me learn by paradox that the way down is the way up, that to be low is to be high, that the broken heart is the healed heart, that the contrite spirit is the rejoicing spirit, that the repenting soul is the victorious soul, that to have nothing is to possess all, that to bear the cross is to wear the crown, that to give is to receive."[6] The prayers in the pages to come are intended to point our children to the "narrow gate" (Matthew 7:13) of Jesus' humility.

From the first moment we lay eyes on our children, we would give them anything. But God can give them even more. "God blesses those who are humble, for they will inherit the whole earth" (Matthew 5:5 NLT).

---

6. Bennett, Arthur, ed. *The Valley of Vision*, p. xxiv.

LIFE BEYOND LABELS

"Should you then seek great things for
 yourself?
Do not seek them."

Jeremiah 45:5

Don't all parents dream their children will do great things, Lord?

Isn't it natural to look at every achievement and accomplishment, and smile?

But there's a lot in a look! Your Word says very plainly that "haughty eyes, a proud heart, and evil actions are all sin" (Proverbs 21:4ª). I have to be careful to want what you want as I dream of what my child might be.

Whoever follows you "will never walk in darkness, but will have the light of life" (John 8:12). My son needs your "light to shine" (John 12:46ᵇ) on him so that he learns to trust you with every step he takes.

There is a difference between seeking great things for himself and seeking them for you. You tell us, "Don't be impressed with your own wisdom" (Proverbs 3:7ᶜ).

After all, "the wisdom of this world is foolishness" to you (1 Corinthians 3:19[d]).

But if he seeks your kingdom "above all else" and lives "righteously" you will give him everything he needs (Matthew 6:33[e]).

I pray that you will keep him free from the "love of money" and help him to "be content" with what he has (Hebrews 13:5), because "the love of money is the root of all kinds of evil. And some people, craving money, have wandered from the true faith and pierced themselves with many sorrows" (1 Timothy 6:10[f]).

I also ask that you give him wisdom to see through the "hollow and deceptive" thinking "which depends on human tradition" and the principles "of this world" instead of you (Colossians 2:8).

Lift him to life beyond labels and titles, Lord. Whatever he may accomplish, may his relationship with you be what matters most!

Teach him "to realize the brevity of life" (Psalm 90:12[g]) so he may use his time on this earth wisely. Life is so short! "Like the morning fog—it's here a little while, then it's gone" (James 4:14[h]).

I pray he will be truly great—a person with a humble heart who loves you and depends on you.

Then he will have a life that accomplishes something, because he'll live in the strength you give and not his own.

You oppose "the proud," but give grace "to the humble" (1 Peter 5:5[i]). Please give him grace to live for more than just himself.

"How great is the goodness you have stored up for those who fear you. You lavish it on those who come to you for protection, blessing them before the watching world. You hide them in the shelter of your presence" (Psalm 31:19–20[j]).

I pray that your favor may rest on him so he may be blessed in all he does.

"Establish the work" of his hands, Lord (Psalm 90:17[k]), so that all he does is for you!

a NLT, b NLT, c NLT, d NKJV, e NLT, f NLT, g NLT, h NLT, i ESV, j NLT, k ESV

BROKEN AND BLESSED

> "I tell you, her sins—and they are many—
> have been forgiven, so she has shown me
> much love. But a person who is forgiven
> little shows only little love."
>
> Luke 7:47 (NLT)

Your forgiveness is beautiful, Lord.

It cost you everything. But all we have to do is ask sincerely, and you "remove our" sins from us "as far as the east is from the west" (Psalm 103:12[a]).

You even tell us you will remember our sins "no more" (Isaiah 43:25)!

No wonder the woman whose many sins you forgave "loved much" (Luke 7:47[b]). How could she not? She knew what you had done for her.

But rich as your "kindness, tolerance and patience" are (Romans 2:4[c]), the human heart "is deceitful above all things and desperately wicked" (Jeremiah 17:9[d]).

How easy it is for our hearts to be "hardened by the deceitfulness of sin" (Hebrews 3:13[e])!

What starts as just a 'small sin' in our eyes—even one 'little' compromise—will take us to dark places where we never thought we would go.

So today I pray for my daughter's heart. I pray her heart will be soft and sensitive to you.

Father, you promised in your Word, "I will give you a new heart, and I will put a new spirit in you. I will take out your stony, stubborn heart and give you a tender, responsive heart. And I will put my Spirit in you so that you will follow" (Ezekiel 36:26–27[f]).

That is what I ask for my daughter, and I praise you that I'm asking for something you have assured us you will give!

Fill her with your Spirit, Lord, so that she loves you and will be free to "walk in your ways" (2 Chronicles 6:31[g]).

Protect her from sin's deceitfulness, so that her mind won't become "dark and confused" (Romans 1:21[h]). Let her be radiant with your joy instead!

I pray she will "be transformed by the renewing" of her mind (Romans 12:2[i]), with her thinking inspired by the genius of your Spirit and your Word instead of our culture's catwalk of conformity that dresses us in chains.

Help her to stay so close to you that she will know the gentle promptings of your Spirit to keep her on your path. May she daily hear you say "This is the way, walk in it" (Isaiah 30:21[j])!

Please give her grace to understand how sin hurts your heart, so she may not "grieve the Holy Spirit" (Ephesians 4:30[k]).

May she love you so much that she wants to stay away from sin!

Lord Jesus, the woman who showed you "much love" (Luke 7:47[1]) may have been broken, but how blessed she was because of it! You told her, "Your faith has saved you; go in peace" (Luke 7:50)!

I pray my daughter will bow before you with the same loving faith and humility, so that she may be saved, sanctified, and set free to walk forever in the beauty of your peace.

a ESV, b ESV, c NASB, d NKJV, e ESV, f NLT, g ESV, h NLT, i NKJV, j ESV, k ESV, l NLT

HEALTHY FEAR

Come, my children, listen to me;
I will teach you the fear of the Lord.

Psalm 34:11

I've tried to teach him to have healthy fear, Father. You've seen each moment . . .

'Look both ways before you cross the street.' 'Don't pet a dog if he's growling.' 'Stay out of the deep end until you know how to swim.'

Some lessons stuck. Some he had to learn the hard way.

I want so much for him to have wisdom that keeps him from harm and blesses him all his life. And that starts with learning to have respect and reverence for you.

Your Word tells us, "The fear of the Lord is the beginning of wisdom" (Psalm 111:10[a]). You even promise to "bless those who fear" you (Psalm 115:13)!

So today I pray my son will both adore you and have a healthy respect for all you are. You are "glorious in holiness, awesome in splendor" (Exodus 15:11[b]). And we are so small and sinful.

"O Lᴏʀᴅ, what are human beings that you should notice them, mere mortals that you should think about them?" (Psalm 144:3ᶜ).

But you do! And in such beautiful and infinitely tender ways: "Even the hairs" of our heads "are all numbered" (Matthew 10:30ᵈ).

Please give my child insight to know that reverence for you shouldn't keep him away. Let it inspire him to draw closer! When he understands that you are both powerful and loving, he will see that you are strong enough to care about the most intimate details of his life, and know that you are "mighty to save" (Isaiah 63:1).

Nothing can stop you, and no one is stronger than you! I ask that you will be his "sure foundation," blessing him with "salvation and wisdom and knowledge." Living with respect for all that you are is "the key to this treasure" (Isaiah 33:6).

I pray that my son will "work hard to show the results" of his salvation, "obeying" you "with deep reverence and fear" (Philippians 2:12ᵉ).

Not out of "fear of punishment"—because then he would not have "fully experienced" your "perfect love" (1 John 4:18ᶠ). I ask that he will learn to love and honor you in all he does and "trust in" you "with all" his heart, instead of depending on his "own understanding" (Proverbs 3:5ᵍ).

Your Word promises that "the fear of the Lᴏʀᴅ leads to life, and whoever has it rests satisfied" (Proverbs 19:23ʰ). Thank you, Father, that when we come to you we do not come "to a place of flaming fire, darkness, gloom, and whirlwind, as the Israelites did at Mount Sinai" (Hebrews 12:18[i]).

Through your Son's kindness to us at the cross, we "have come to Mount Zion, to the city of the living God, the heavenly Jerusalem." We "have come to thousands upon thousands of angels in joyful assembly" (Hebrews 12:22).

Oh to be part of that! To join all of heaven in your praise together, saying, "Holy, holy, holy is the Lord God Almighty, who was and is and is to come!" (Revelation 4:8[j]).

a ESV, b NLT, c NLT, d ESV, e NLT, f NLT, g ESV, h ESV, i NLT, j NKJV

CONSTRUCTIVE CRITICISM

> If you listen to constructive criticism, you
>   will be at home
> among the wise. If you reject discipline,
>   you only harm yourself;
> but if you listen to correction, you grow in
>   understanding.
>
> Proverbs 15:31–32 (NLT)

I pray that my child will learn to accept "constructive criticism," Father (Proverbs 15:31[a]).

He will need to "listen to advice and accept instruction" (Proverbs 19:20[b]), if he is going to do well at home or at school or at work.

So today I ask that he will be able to "accept correction" (Zephaniah 3:7[c]) with grace—grace that flows out of a loving relationship with you.

If he takes to heart the truth that you love and accept him unconditionally, it will make his learning and growing that much easier.

But listening to constructive criticism isn't easy! It takes humility, wisdom, maturity, and faith!

So I pray he will be humble enough to intently "listen to correction" (Proverbs 15:32^d), understanding that "with humility comes wisdom" (Proverbs 11:2).

I also ask that you give him the wisdom to "test" whether what he hears is genuinely from you (1 John 4:1^e), or if it is simply offered in a critical spirit not intended to help. Please guide him so that he can "reject the wrong and choose the right" (Isaiah 7:15)!

When he has willfully "strayed from your path" (Psalm 44:18), please help him to have the strength to "repent" and "turn away from" all his "offenses" (Ezekiel 18:30). Your Word says that "a rebuke impresses a discerning person" (Proverbs 17:10) and I pray that he will be one!

I thank you that you will encourage him as he walks with you, Lord. May he be "mature and fully assured" (Colossians 4:12^f) so that he is strong enough to learn from his mistakes.

Your Word teaches us that if you "reprove the wise" they "will love you" (Proverbs 9:8^g). I pray he will have that kind of heart!

Please give him the ability to step back and look at himself without being defensive, so that he can realize those areas in which he needs to improve.

When the learning curve is steep and life is difficult, I pray that he will have the faith and humility to persevere and stay close to you, because you "lead the humble in doing right"(Psalm 25:9^h).

When you seem distant and he cannot see your hand at work, I ask that you will help him to trust in your love, because you are "the faithful one" (Isaiah 49:7ⁱ).

Please give him a desire for excellence so that he will be "truly competent" in his life and work (Proverbs 22:29[j]). You created him to love you in everything he does; I pray he will serve and represent you well!

I praise you that you "will work out" your "plans" for his life—"for your faithful love, O Lord, endures forever" (Psalm 138:8[k])!

a NLT, b ESV, c ESV, d NLT, e ESV, f ESV, g ESV, h NLT, i NLT, j NLT, k NLT

THIRD PLACE WINS!

"You know that the rulers in this world lord
it over their people, and officials flaunt
their authority over those under them.
But among you it will be different. Whoever wants to be a leader among you
must be your servant, and whoever wants
to be first among you must be the slave
of everyone else. For even the Son of Man
came not to be served but to serve others
and to give his life as a ransom for many."

Mark 10:42–45 (NLT)

I suppose it is human nature to want "to be first" (3 John 9),
isn't it Lord?

But it's not your nature, Jesus.

You "came not to be served but to serve others" and to give
your life "as a ransom for many" (Mark 10:45[a]).

Even though you "and the father are one" (John 10:30[b]), you
"did not think of equality with God as something to
cling to." Instead, you "gave up" your "divine privileges."

You "took the humble position of a slave" and were "born as a human being" (Philippians 2:6–7[c]).

You even "died a criminal's death on a cross" (Philippians 2:8[d])!

Your humility is awe-inspiring, Lord, and I worship you for it!

You didn't have to do these things. No one made you. You simply did them out of love.

Today I pray that my child will be so much like you that she will want to serve others as well.

Your Word tells how you were "moved with compassion" (Mark 1:41[e]), Lord Jesus. I pray that your compassion will fill my child's heart and mind as well.

In a world that says we should put ourselves first, I pray that she will see the beauty of putting herself third—simply for the joy of serving you and loving others.

I pray that she will feel a special closeness to you as she helps others in need, understanding that she is somehow caring for you at the same time. Isn't that how you described it, Jesus? You said, "Whatever you did for one of the least of these . . . you did for me" (Matthew 25:40).

You said that third place wins . . . that "the last will be first, and the first last" (Matthew 20:16[f])!

As I pray that my child will love third place, I know I also need to ask this for myself.

Please help me to set an example for her in serving and loving like you. Then she will see you in me, because you promise that others "will know that" we belong to you if we genuinely "love one another" (John 13:35).

There's no limit to your love, Lord! How "great is your love, higher than the heavens; your faithfulness reaches to the skies" (Psalm 108:4)!

You "live in a high and holy place," but also with those who are "contrite and lowly in spirit" (Isaiah 57:15). The scope of your love is breathtaking, and I praise you for it!

Please help us to "humble" ourselves before you, so that you "will lift" us up (James 4:10)!

a NLT, b ESV, c NLT, d NLT, e NASB, f ESV

BLESSED BY DISCIPLINE

> My child, don't reject the Lord's discipline,
>   and don't be upset
> when he corrects you. For the Lord
>   corrects those he loves,
> just as a father corrects a child in whom
>   he delights.
>
> Proverbs 3:11–12 (NLT)

I pray for my son in those moments when you will have to discipline him, Father.

Discipline is never easy. "No discipline seems pleasant at the time, but painful." But afterwards "it produces a harvest of righteousness and peace for those who have been trained by it" (Hebrews 12:11).

Every time you disciplined me you were right to do it. There were times when I willfully strayed from your path and you corrected me and showed me "the consequences" of my actions (Ezekiel 44:10). Yet you didn't do it in anger, you did it in love, just as a "father corrects a child in whom he delights" (Proverbs 3:12[a]).

But it was tough! Sometimes I felt like you were angry. I'm reminded of David's prayer: "LORD, do not rebuke me in your anger or discipline me in your wrath. . . . My soul is in anguish. How long, LORD, how long? Turn, LORD, and deliver me; save me because of your unfailing love" (Psalm 6:1, 3–4).

There were times when you felt so far away, and other times when "your hand of discipline was heavy on me," and "my strength evaporated like water in the summer heat" (Psalm 32:4[b]).

"When you hid your face, I was dismayed" (Psalm 30:7), but then "I acknowledged my sin to you," and "you forgave" me (Psalm 32:5).

I know there are times when my son will need to confess his sins and ask your forgiveness as well, Lord Jesus.

You are "the one who is truly righteous" and "the sacrifice that atones for our sins" (1 John 2:1–2[c]). I praise you that we are forgiven because of all you have done for us!

But I also know that there are times when my son will sin and face consequences, because your Word tells us that "everyone undergoes discipline" (Hebrews 12:8). If we do not, we "are not really" your "children at all" (Hebrews 12:8[d]).

So I pray that he will not "make light" of your "discipline" or "give up" when you correct him (Hebrews 12:5[e]).

I ask that he will have a humble heart that is quick to confess his sin with "godly sorrow" that "brings repentance" (2 Corinthians 7:10), so that he follows you with new faithfulness.

I praise you, Father, because your discipline is perfect. You discipline "the one" you love (Hebrews 12:6[f]), and we are blessed as a result.

Your discipline "is always good for us, so that we might share in" your "holiness" (Hebrews 12:10[g]). "Joyful are those you discipline, LORD, those you teach with your instructions" (Psalm 94:12[h]).

I pray my child will "submit" to you, "the Father of our spirits" and "live" (Hebrews 12:9)!

Day 63

"I DID IT"

> If we confess our sins, he is faithful and just
> and will forgive us our sins and purify us
> from all unrighteousness.
>
> 1 John 1:9

I pray that my child will be humble enough to admit when she is wrong, Father. Sometimes that's so hard for us to do!

I think of Adam 'passing the buck' when he ate the forbidden fruit. When you asked him about it, he told you, "The woman you put here with me—she gave me some fruit from the tree, and I ate it" (Genesis 3:12).

And I think of Eve doing the same thing. She told you, "The serpent deceived me, and I ate" (Genesis 3:13).

Both of their responses remind me of the countless times I have done the same thing, blaming my sins on others even when I knew in my own heart I was wrong.

Thank you for your patience with us, Father, and for helping us understand "your way" (Psalm 27:11ª). I praise you that because of your mercy we can genuinely grow and leave old sins behind us!

You tell us in your Word, "My thoughts are not your thoughts, neither are your ways my ways" (Isaiah 55:8[b]). How we need you to "show" us "your ways" (Psalm 25:4), Lord!

Today I pray that my daughter will learn to love humility and to accept responsibility for the things she does wrong.

Please help her to understand that admitting her sins and faults doesn't make her less of a person—it makes her more of one in your eyes. Your Word tells us that "humility comes before honor" (Proverbs 15:33[c]), and that you "beautify the humble with salvation" (Psalm 149:4[d]).

I pray that the beauty of your Spirit will rest upon her so that she walks before you with "integrity of heart and uprightness" (1 Kings 9:4[e]).

"I know, my God, that you examine our hearts and rejoice when you find integrity there" (1 Chronicles 29:17[f]). May she bring you joy again and again!

I ask that her integrity will be rooted in her relationship with you and not in self-righteousness, because "no one living is righteous before you" (Psalm 143:2).

"It is through the grace of our Lord Jesus that we are saved" (Acts 15:11), and "if anyone thinks he is something, when he is nothing, he deceives himself" (Galatians 6:3[g]).

I understand there are times when admitting she is wrong may cost her in the world's eyes, Lord. But only your eyes matter, and they see her "every step" (Job 34:21).

You are able to care for her and provide for her no matter what may happen. You "make the righteous secure" (Psalm 7:9).

I pray that her "soul finds rest" in you, because her "salvation comes from" you (Psalm 62:1).

Resting in you, she will be truly secure—even secure enough to admit her faults! Your Word declares that "people who conceal their sins will not prosper, but if they confess and turn from them, they will receive mercy" (Proverbs 28:13[h]).

May she always live in your mercy, Lord—and always love you for it!

a ESV, b ESV, c ESV, d NKJV, e ESV, f NLT, g ESV, h NLT

Week 10

PURE

"Tag, You're It!"

> "Blessed are the pure in heart, for they will see God."
>
> Matthew 5:8

Innocence is a gift from God. The wide eyes and open hearts of childhood remind us that we were created by someone who "is righteous in everything he does" and "is filled with kindness" (Psalm 145:17 NLT).

But how we change with time. Hands close and hearts along with them—even to the point of shaking our fists at the sky. Once innocence is lost, can you ever get it back again?

Jesus answers that question in an unexpected place—the middle of a graveyard, where "day and night" a man wanders naked among the tombs, "howling and cutting himself with sharp stones" (Mark 5:5 NLT).

He was once a mother's baby, but that was years before. Now he was the one his family mentioned only in whispers, if they spoke of him at all. We still don't know his name.

When Jesus asked for his name, the man answered, "My name is Legion . . . for we are many" (Mark 5:9).

But that wasn't his real name, and Jesus knew it. By the time Jesus finished with the man, he would be "sitting there" at Jesus' feet, "fully clothed and perfectly sane" (Mark 5:15 NLT).

You might think the story is finished there, but it's really only beginning. Jesus didn't just set the man free from a "legion of demons" (Mark 5:15). The man "begged to go with" Jesus (Mark 5:18), but the Lord instead sent him on a mission—even before He "began sending" the disciples (Mark 6:7 NLT). Jesus told the man, "Go home to your own people and tell them how much the Lord has done for you, and how he has had mercy on you" (Mark 5:19).

The man did what Jesus told him to do . . . and more. Mark tells us that "the man started off to visit the Ten Towns of that region and began to proclaim the great things Jesus had done for him; and everyone was amazed at what he told them" (Mark 5:20 NLT).

You can only imagine those conversations. People used to cross the street when they saw this man coming. But now, instead of gnashing his teeth at others, he smiles and says, "No, it's alright. Please come back. I have some really good news to share with you!"

He apparently had an impact. The next time Jesus visited this predominantly non-Jewish area, the people—instead of "pleading" with him "to go away and leave them alone" (Mark 5:17 NLT)—"brought to him a man who was deaf and could hardly talk" (Mark 7:32). Then a crowd of "about 4,000 people" gathered (Mark 8:9 NLT).

So there you have it. A wasted, howling wreck of a man once known as "Legion" was transformed into one of history's first missionaries—and a highly effective one. All because he "ran to" Jesus (Mark 5:6), who is innocence found.

Who knows the effect this man had on lives over time? His story makes me think of the one we used to tell as kids. We spoke of a horrible monster that would chase you until you had nowhere else to run. Then he would reach out his scary hand and say . . . "Tag, you're it!"

Jesus touched a man's life, the man touched others, and they touched others, and . . . who knows? Maybe twenty-one centuries later, one of them touched you and me.

Now it's time to "tag" our kids, and point them back to Jesus. This week we're praying our children will discover the innocence only He can give. When we run to Jesus, He can forgive "our sins and purify us from all unrighteousness" (1 John 1:9). He can clean us up from the muck of the world so that we are "pure in heart" (Matthew 5:8), discovering life with fresh, new purpose. This week we'll pray that our children will "keep" themselves "in God's love" as they "wait for the mercy of our Lord Jesus Christ" to bring them "to eternal life" (Jude 21), and live in such a way that they may be deeply blessed.

These are prayers to address the effects of what has been called the "unholy trinity" of "the world, the flesh and the devil"[7] on our children. Nothing can stand against our Savior's love. Greater is he who is in us than he "who is in the world" (1 John 4:4).

---

7.   J. C. Ryle, from the tract, "Are You Fighting?"

CATCH HER DRIFT

Don't let me drift toward evil.

Psalm 141:4 (NLT)

It can happen so easily, Father.

The world turns on its way and we go along with it unaware.

Like a swimmer in a current who turns and finds herself farther from shore than she ever meant to be, how easily we can "drift toward evil" (Psalm 141:4ᵃ) and find ourselves far from you.

Catch her drift, Lord. Don't let her be swept up in the world's ways, because "this world as we know it will soon pass away" (1 Corinthians 7:31ᵇ).

But "anyone who listens" to your teaching and follows it "is wise, like a person who builds a house on solid rock. Though the rain comes in torrents and the floodwaters rise and the winds beat against that house, it won't collapse because it is built on bedrock" (Matthew 7:24–25ᶜ).

I praise you, Jesus, that you save us from destruction as we turn to you. Because of your "great love we are not consumed"; your "compassions never fail" (Lamentations 3:22)!

I pray her life will be built on all that you are. Help her to learn her values from your Word, not from worldly friends or the media, or the ever-shifting sands of the culture around us. Make her holy "by your truth," Father. "Your word is truth" (John 17:17[d]).

Help her to discern the difference between right and wrong through the gentle prompting of your Holy Spirit.

Thank you that you have "sent the Spirit" of your Son "into our hearts, prompting us to call out, 'Abba, Father!'" (Galatians 4:6[e]).

Abba, "My prayer is not that you take" her "out of the world but that you protect" her "from the evil one" (John 17:15).

Strengthen her by your Spirit in her "inner being" (Ephesians 3:16[f]) so that she will have the wisdom to "keep away from worldly desires which wage war" against her very soul (1 Peter 2:11[g]).

Keep her from the pain and emptiness that happen when we're "drawn away" by our "own evil desire and enticed" (James 1:14).

I pray she will be "filled with love that comes from a pure heart, a clear conscience, and genuine faith" (1 Timothy 1:5[h]).

Give her grace to "run from anything that stimulates youthful lusts," and help her to "instead, pursue righteous living, faithfulness, love, and peace" (2 Timothy 2:22[i]).

Please also give her close, believing friends so that she may "enjoy the companionship of those who call on the Lord with pure hearts" (2 Timothy 2:22[j]).

Let them look forward to you together, each day "encouraging one another" (Hebrews 10:25) in you, who are always worthy to receive "honor and glory and praise!" (Revelation 5:12).

a NLT, b NLT, c NLT, d NKJV, e NLT, f ESV, g NLT, h NLT, i NLT, j NLT

WASH YOUR HANDS!

Come close to God, and God will come close to you. Wash your hands, you sinners; purify your hearts, for your loyalty is divided between God and the world.

James 4:8 (NLT)

Father, when I think about how holy you are, I have to think of what Isaiah said: "I am a man of unclean lips, and I live among a people of unclean lips" (Isaiah 6:5).

If you didn't save me, I would be completely "lost" (Isaiah 6:5[a])!

But you have saved me. You saved me "not because of righteous things" I had done, "but because of" your "mercy" (Titus 3:5).

I praise you for "such a great salvation" (Hebrews 2:3[b])!

The only reason we can love you is that you loved us "first" (1 John 4:19[c]). That makes me want to love you even more. And when I get closer to you, you come closer to me!

Father, I pray that my child will deeply desire to be close to you, and ask that your Spirit move in his heart "for this very purpose" (2 Corinthians 5:5).

I taught him how to wash his hands, but only you can wash his heart.

Only you can clean us up from all of our sins, and only you know how deeply stained we are. Even "our righteous acts are like filthy rags" before you (Isaiah 64:6).

"Who can say, 'I have kept my heart pure; I am clean and without sin?'" (Proverbs 20:9).

But you never give up on us! After you save us your Spirit continues to change us, helping us grow and showing us those places where our "loyalty is divided" between you "and the world" (James 4:8d).

You keep on scrubbing! You gently tell us, "Come now, let us reason together . . . though your sins are like scarlet, they shall be as white as snow" (Isaiah 1:18e).

You even help us to want what you want! You love us with "an everlasting love" that goes soul deep, drawing us near with an "unfailing kindness" (Jeremiah 31:3) that defies human logic and becomes our very reason for living.

Oh, Father! I pray my son will cherish your invincible, uncontainable love, and "honor" you "as holy" in his heart (Numbers 20:12).

I pray he will have a heart that is sensitive to sin, one that learns to love what you love. May your love make him bold—bold enough to know he can leave old sins behind and genuinely change, walking with you in fresh innocence.

May he be mature enough to admit when he's wrong, and quick to "seek reconciliation" with you and others (Proverbs 14:9f).

I pray he will always understand that "we do not make requests of you because we are righteous, but because of your great mercy" (Daniel 9:18).

May the cry of his heart be, "Wash me," Lord, "and I shall be clean" (Psalm 51:7^g)!

Then with "clean hands and a pure heart" (Psalm 24:4^h), he will live in the joy of your presence forever!

a ESV, b ESV, c NKJV, d NLT, e ESV, f NLT, g ESV, h ESV

FOR FRIENDS

Whoever walks with the wise becomes
wise,
but the companion of fools will suffer
harm.

Proverbs 13:20 (ESV)

When I think of the influence the right friends can have in my child's life, Father, it makes me want to ask you for them.

I pray for close friendships with good, believing friends so they may "encourage one another daily" in their faith in you (Hebrews 3:13).

Let them "encourage one another and build each other up" (1 Thessalonians 5:11) so they may live strong, effective lives for you.

I think about how Paul described his friend Timothy: "I have no one else like him, who will show genuine concern" in others, not for his own purposes, but for "those of Jesus Christ" (Philippians 2:20–21).

Paul was inspired by a friend who clearly loved you and served you.

That's what I want for my daughter! A friend like that is a precious gift of eternal worth.

I pray for friends who will have a contagious, winsome faith, so they may "motivate one another to acts of love and good works" (Hebrews 10:24[a]).

Your Word says that "a friend loves at all times" (Proverbs 17:17[b]), so I ask you will give her friends who will love her unconditionally, celebrating her strengths and patiently bearing with her faults.

But I also pray for friends who will speak "the truth in love" (Ephesians 4:13[c]) and help her reach for her best, because "as iron sharpens iron, so a friend sharpens a friend" (Proverbs 27:17[d]). "Faithful are the wounds of a friend" (Proverbs 27:5–6[e]) who loves enough to tell the truth—even when it hurts.

Lord Jesus, I pray you will keep her from the hurt and harm foolish friends can cause; may she "walk with the wise and become wise" (Proverbs 13:20[f])!

Protect her, Lord, from friends who give no thought to you, who think "only about having a good time" (Ecclesiastes 7:4[g]). Your Word is clear on the fact that "bad company corrupts good character" (1 Corinthians 15:33)!

Please keep her from those who may appear to be wise but do not honor you "as God or give thanks" to you, "futile in their thinking" (Romans 1:21[h]) that human knowledge reigns supreme. "The world" does not know you "through its wisdom" (1 Corinthians 1:21)!

But she can know you through your kindness! When you "our Savior revealed" your "kindness and love," you "saved us, not because of the righteous things we had done," but because of your "mercy." You "washed away our sins, giving us a new birth and new life through the Holy Spirit" (Titus 3:4–5[i]).

May your Spirit give life to her in her friendships, Lord!

You know how to make friendship work better than anyone else. "Greater love has no one than this, that someone lay down his life for his friends" (John 15:13[j]).

She could never have a better friend than you!

a NLT, b ESV, c ESV, d NLT, e ESV, f NLT, g NLT, h ESV, i NLT, j ESV

A SHINING STAR

Do everything without complaining or arguing, so that you may become blameless and pure, "children of God without fault in a warped and crooked generation." Then you will shine among them like stars in the sky as you hold firmly to the word of life.

Philippians 2:14–16

So many people want their kids to be stars, Lord. I see it everywhere . . . in pageants and programs and athletic events.

If I'm honest, I have to admit that sometimes I want my child to be a star as well. But I ask for grace to want this in a different way: I pray that he will shine for you.

So I begin by asking that you, "the morning star" will rise in his heart (2 Peter 1:19[a]). I pray that he will know you and be a shining example of your love in this dark world. May others see you in him because he follows you closely and lives transparently.

I also ask that he will keep himself "from being polluted by the world" (James 1:27), and that you will help him to "stay pure" by "obeying your Word" (Psalm 119:9[b]).

May he be so in love with you that you fill his mind and heart! Help him to fix his "thoughts on what is true, and honorable, and right, and pure, and lovely, and admirable" (Philippians 4:8[c])—you are all of those things!

Let your love be so evident in him that it shows up on his face and radiates from the words he says and the things he does. May he have so much joy because of what you have done for him that he lives enthusiastically for you, "without complaining or arguing" (Philippians 2:14).

May his love for you exude from "a pure heart and a good conscience and a sincere faith" (1 Timothy 1:5[d]).

I pray that you will empower him to "hold firmly to the word of life" (Philippians 2:16) in such a way that others will be drawn to you, Lord Jesus. Your Word tells us that "those who lead many to righteousness will shine like the stars forever" (Daniel 12:3[e]).

Let him shine, Lord! May he know the joy of seeing others come to you!

Let him be there in that moment when dawn breaks and you, "the bright morning star" (Revelation 22:16[f]), shine with power in a life where darkness once reigned.

Let him see the miracle only you can do in a soul, and praise you for it!

"Send out your light and your truth; let them lead" him (Psalm 43:3[g]), Lord! Let them lead him into your presence and your peace every day.

Your "light shines on the godly, and joy on those whose hearts are right" (Psalm 97:11[h]). May his heart be right with you!

I pray for "faith" that "is flourishing" and "love" that "is growing" (2 Thessalonians 1:3[i]) day by day.

You do "great things too marvelous to understand." Every day you perform "countless miracles" (Job 9:10[j])!

I pray my son will know the joy of seeing you move in his life and the lives of others, and take in with breathless wonder the beauty of heaven touching earth.

a ESV, b NLT, c NLT, d ESV, e NLT, f ESV, g ESV, h NLT, i NLT, j NLT

DESIRES

Take delight in the LORD, and he will give
   you your heart's desires.
Commit everything you do to the LORD.
   Trust him, and he will help you.
He will make your innocence radiate like
   the dawn,
and the justice of your cause will shine like
   the noonday sun.

Psalm 37:4–6 (NLT)

What you do with our desires is beautiful, Lord.

When we "take delight in" you, you give us our "hearts' desires" (Psalm 37:4ᵃ).

It's not that you give us whatever we want. You give us new and right desires . . . and then you fulfill them!

Only you can give us real and lasting satisfaction in life. We were made for you, and you know better than anyone else what will make us happy.

So today I pray for my child's desires and ask that you work in them.

I ask that you will give her wisdom be able to "discern what is pleasing" to you (Ephesians 5:10[b]), and make that her goal for life.

"Every good and perfect gift" is from you; you do not change like the "shifting shadows" (James 1:17) of this world. You give what is original and best! Please help her not to be tripped up by the devil's counterfeits.

I pray she "will learn to know" your "will" for her, because it is "good and pleasing and perfect" (Romans 12:2[c]).

Help her to live for you without compromise, and "put to death" the things that belong to her "earthly nature: sexual immorality, impurity, lust, evil desires and greed, which is idolatry. Because of these," your wrath "is coming" (Colossians 3:5–6)!

Please give her the discernment to understand how important it is to walk closely with you in every area of life, so that she might "cling to" her "faith in Christ" and keep her "conscience clear" (1 Timothy 1:19[d]).

Only you can help her win her battles, Lord! You "fulfill the desire of those who fear" you; you "hear their cry and save them" (Psalm 145:19[e]).

Please give her grace not to compartmentalize her life and just give you part of it. I pray she will "clothe" herself with your "presence," Lord Jesus, and not let herself "think about ways to indulge" sinful desires (Romans 13:14[f]).

When that means she needs to make tough choices, I pray she will do what is right—instead of enjoying "the passing pleasures of sin" (Hebrews 11:25[g]).

I praise you that we really can make the right choices and leave old sins behind us, because "through the power of the Spirit" we can "put to death the deeds" of our "sinful nature" (Romans 8:13[h]).

May "the Spirit renew" her "thoughts and attitudes," so she can "put on" her "new nature, created to be like" you—"truly righteous and holy" (Ephesians 4:23–24[i]).

"The mind governed by the Spirit is life and peace" (Romans 8:6). Help her to live with her heart at peace with you!

You satisfy our "desires with good things" (Psalm 103:5). I pray she will live celebrating the happiness you alone can give!

a NLT, b ESV, c NLT, d NLT, e NKJV, f NLT, g NKJV, h NLT, i NLT

CROUCHING SIN AND SINGING ANGELS

"Sin is crouching at your door; it desires to
have you, but you must rule over it."

Genesis 4:7

There it is, lurking in the shadows . . . the same old sin that
has tripped her up before.

She knows better. But she does it anyway.

I'm afraid the forbidden fruit doesn't fall too far from the
family tree. "Everyone has sinned; we all fall short" of
your "glorious standard" (Romans 3:23ᵃ).

I think of the number of times I have been stuck in a rut
with a sin; sometimes it took me years to truly turn
from my sin and grow beyond it!

But your kindness to me through it all was amazing. You
were "patient" with me and never gave up on me, always
wanting me "to come to repentance" (2 Peter 3:9).

I praise you, Father, because even when "we are not faithful," you "will remain faithful" (2 Timothy 2:13ᵇ).

I thank you, Lord Jesus, that because of your cross, "my
interest in this world has been crucified, and the world's

interest in me has also died." Lord, "may I never boast about anything except" your cross (Galatians 6:14[c])!

I love you, Holy Spirit, because even though my actions grieved you, you continued to "teach" me and "remind" me of my Savior's love and teaching (John 14:26).

Today I ask you to bless my daughter with the joy that comes from repenting.

Lord Jesus, you said that "there is joy in the presence of God's angels when even one sinner repents" (Luke 15:10[d]). So where there is sin in her life I pray she will have a change of heart that makes the angels sing!

May your light that "produces only what is good, right and true" (Ephesians 5:9[e]) shine into her heart to dispel the darkness—then radiate from her face in love for you and all you have done.

Please give my daughter the grace to understand that she will never be truly happy apart from you!

I pray she will come to understand that she doesn't have to stay stuck in old ways because real progress is possible with you. You came "to proclaim freedom for the captives and release from darkness for the prisoners" (Isaiah 61:1).

When "sin is crouching" (Genesis 4:7) at the door of her heart, I pray she will let you answer the door!

Set her free, Lord Jesus! Free to live to please you! Please break the chains that bind her so she may follow you, rejoicing! When the angels sing, let her sing too!

May she live in such a way that you will love to bless her. You "will withhold no good thing from those who do what is right" (Psalm 84:11[f]).

May she know the soul-satisfying sight of old sins in the rearview mirror, fading in the distance . . . then gone for good.

Then she will see the land of your promise and peace ahead, nearer and brighter every day.

a NLT, b NIrV, c NLT, d NLT, e NLT, f NLT

Day 70

KNOCK, KNOCK . . .

"I correct and discipline everyone I love.
So be diligent and turn from your indiffer-
ence. Look! I stand at the door and knock.
If you hear my voice and open the door,
I will come in, and we will share a meal
together as friends."

Revelation 3:19–20 (NLT)

Lord Jesus, even though your Word tells us you are "near" (Philippians 4:5), sometimes we can be so far away.

You know better than anyone how easily we can be distracted. No matter how much we may love you, we
always need to love you more!

So today I pray that you will protect my child from indifference, and help him to keep his focus on you.

I ask that he will "never be lacking in zeal" but will keep
his "spiritual fervor," loving and "serving" you (Romans
12:11) as long as he lives.

May you be his "first love" (Revelation 2:4ᵃ)—the highest
priority of his life.

I'm reminded that when you said, "I stand at the door and knock" (Revelation 3:20), you were talking to people in the church who already knew you! They were saying, "I am rich. I have everything I want. I don't need a thing!" (Revelation 3:17[b]).

But because of their love of material things, they were spiritually "neither hot nor cold" (Revelation 3:16[c]). They were "wretched and miserable and poor and blind and naked," and didn't even "realize" it (Revelation 3:17[d]).

I pray you will keep my son "from idols" (1 John 5:21[e]) and the indifference that creeps in when we love material things too much.

Please give him the sensitivity to your Spirit to understand that anything that occupies his affections more than you is an idol.

I pray that nothing (and no one) will take the place in his heart that you deserve. Your Word teaches us the hard truth that "if anyone loves the world, the love of the Father is not in him" (1 John 2:15[f]).

When the world around him tells him that he needs this or that thing to 'be someone,' please remind him that he already has all he needs. When we receive you, we are your "children" and "heirs" to every good thing (Romans 8:17[g])!

Your Word also tells us clearly that when we "use the things of the world" we "should not become attached to them" (1 Corinthians 7:31[h]). So I ask that he will hold his possessions lightly and use them for your purposes.

May he have the perspective that every good thing he enjoys is a gift from you, and praise you for it!

Help him to understand that it is "better to have little" with devotion to you, "than to have great treasure and inner turmoil" (Proverbs 15:16[i]). Only you can fill the emptiness inside of us!

So I pray that when my child hears you knocking at his heart's door, he will answer every time . . . 'Come in, Lord, and make yourself at home!'

a NKJV, b NLT, c ESV, d NLT, e ESV, f ESV, g NLT, h NLT, i NLT

Week 11

HOPEFUL

Peter's Angel?

No one has yet believed in God and the
Kingdom of God, no one has yet heard
about the realm of the resurrected, and
not been homesick from that hour,
waiting and looking forward joyfully.

Dietrich Bonhoeffer

Sometimes when God answers prayer we have trouble
believing it.

Peter's story comes to mind. The early church was under
heavy persecution in Jerusalem. Herod Agrippa had just
executed "James (John's brother)" and also "arrested Peter"
(Acts 12:2–3 NLT). Herod wasn't about to let his prized pris-
oner get away—Peter was "guarded by four squads of four
soldiers each" (Acts 12:4). But the night before he was to
stand trial, "the church was earnestly praying to God for
him" (Acts 12:5).

God sent an angel to set Peter free. But Peter "had no
idea that what the angel was doing was really happening; he
thought he was seeing a vision" (Acts 12:9). And when he

got to the house where the church is praying, the girl who answered the door was so excited she didn't even let him in. When she told the others, "Peter is at the door!" they answered, "You're out of your mind." But when she "kept insisting," they said, "It must be his angel." The meaning of that comment is unclear, but they may have simply been making light of what the girl was saying. Meanwhile, Peter "kept on knocking" (Acts 12:14–16).

That story gives me hope. It helps me to know that even the first Christians sometimes didn't recognize an answer to prayer when it was standing right in front of them. There have been too many times in my life where I've prayed about something and then, when it happened, I forgot I'd asked for it. Or, like the people who were praying for Peter, I tried to explain away the answer. Still, "the Spirit helps us in our weakness" (Romans 8:26). I take comfort in the fact that God answers prayer even when our asking is less than perfect. And He's patient with us when it takes a while for us to recognize what He has done.

Well over a year after God freed my son from the prison of substance abuse, I was still deeply worried about the possibility of his falling back into it. Though I had seen God work in his life in a powerful way—though I had seen him return to his childhood faith—I kept looking for something bad to happen. "Remember," I warned him, "we have an adversary who is powerful."

"You're right, Dad," he answered. "The devil has power. But he has no authority."

In that moment I knew that my son was in God's hands, and that God could be trusted with the outcome. "All authority in heaven and on earth has been given" to Jesus (Matthew 28:18).

How good it is to know, as David put it, that "The LORD is like a father to his children, tender and compassionate" (Psalm 103:13 NLT). Because He is, we can pray with faith and be encouraged that He will answer in His own time and way.

In the following pages you'll find prayers to send ahead to those places in our children's lives where mistakes are made and worry and discouragement take their toll. Even there, Jesus is Lord. And because He is, we can always hope . . . and we have something to look forward to.

We can look forward to Him.

YES!

For all of God's promises have been ful-
filled in Christ with a resounding "Yes!"
And through Christ, our "Amen" (which
means "Yes") ascends to God for his glory.
2 Corinthians 1:20 (NLT)

Father, as I think about all the times I've had to tell my child 'no' (often for very good reasons!), I praise you for all the times you have told us 'yes'—for the best reason of all.

I praise you for your Son! "No matter how many promises" you have made, "they are 'Yes'" in Him (2 Corinthians 1:20)!

You have given us your "very great and precious promises, so that through them" we "may participate in the divine nature and escape the corruption in the world caused by evil desires" (2 Peter 1:4).

You are so amazing, God! Through your unlimited power you have "given us everything we need for a godly life" (2 Peter 1:3), through the loving blessing of a relation-ship with you.

I pray today that you, "the source of hope, will fill" my child "completely with joy and peace" because she trusts in you. Then she "will overflow with confident hope through the power of the Holy Spirit" (Romans 15:13[a]).

When she asks, 'Does God care about me?', may she hear your Spirit whisper in her heart, "Yes, I have loved you with an everlasting love" (Jeremiah 31:3[b]).

When she wonders how you could possibly forgive her past, may she come to understand the wonder of your assurance of unconditional love: "I—yes, I alone—will blot out your sins for my own sake and will never think of them again" (Isaiah 43:25[c]).

When she finds herself lonely or discouraged, may the gentle joy of your presence in her heart affirm, "I, yes I, am the one who comforts you" (Isaiah 51:12[d]).

And when the world tries to tell her there is another way, may she know that "there is no other God—there never has been, and there never will be." May she know the truth of your promise in her heart, "I, yes I, am the LORD, and there is no other Savior" (Isaiah 43:10–11[e]).

I praise you, Lord Jesus, for what you have done for us! Even though we "were once far away from" the Father, "separated from him" by our "evil thoughts and actions," we have now been "reconciled" through your death for us on the cross. We have even been brought "into his own presence," where we are "holy and blameless" as we "stand before him without a single fault" (Colossians 1:21–22[f]).

May my daughter always love you and humbly follow you. Only you give us lasting hope. Your name is "the hope of all the world" (Matthew 12:21[g])!

I pray she will "hold tightly without wavering to the hope we affirm," because you "can be trusted to keep" your promise (Hebrews 10:23[h]).

Because you have said 'Yes!' to her in all of these things, may she joyfully say 'Yes!' to you!

ANGEL BY THE HAND

With the coming of dawn, the angels
  urged Lot, saying, "Hurry!
Take your wife and your two daughters
  who are here, or you will be swept
  away
when the city is punished." When he hesitated, the men grasped his hand
and the hands of his wife and of his two
  daughters and led them
safely out of the city, for the Lord was merciful to them.

Genesis 19:15–16

The way you saved Lot was amazing, Father.

He was living in Sodom with evil all around. Yet he still didn't want to leave. So you sent your angels to pull him and his family out of harm's way.

When I think of some of the near misses and close calls I've had in my life, I wonder how many times you've done that for me.

I may never know the answer to that question this side of heaven, but I do know this: Your Word tells me that Abraham "drew near" to you interceding for Lot (Genesis 18:23ᵃ) before the angels "grasped" his nephew by the hand (Genesis 19:16).

So today I pray for your angels to protect my child—and I thank you for them!

"Are not all angels ministering spirits sent to serve those who will inherit salvation?" (Hebrews 1:14).

I especially pray for those moments when my child—just like Lot—doesn't have the wisdom to get out of the way.

Please help him, Lord! Send your angels to grab him by the hand and pull him to the place he needs to be.

I ask that you give my son wisdom to run to you and "make" you his "refuge." Your Word tells us plainly that if we make you, "the Most High," our shelter, "no evil will conquer" us. This is because you "will order" your angels "to protect" us wherever we go (Psalm 91:9–11ᵇ).

Father, you also tell us, "I will rescue those who love me. I will protect those who trust in my name. When they call on me, I will answer; I will be with them in trouble. I will rescue and honor them. I will reward them with a long life and give them my salvation" (Psalm 91:14–16ᶜ).

Yes, Lord! May he trust in you and call on you every day! May he fully understand that you alone can save us, body and soul. There is no greater blessing than you!

You are completely trustworthy. Because "it is impossible" for you "to lie," when we run to you for refuge we have "strong encouragement" and "hope" because of your Son (Hebrews 6:18ᵈ)!

Lord Jesus, I pray my son will have the "knowledge of the truth that leads to godliness," and a "faith" that rests "in the hope of eternal life" (Titus 1:1–2).

I pray that he will boldly trust you and confess to others that you are his Savior. If he does that, you promised that you will even "acknowledge" him "before the angels" (Luke 12:8ᵉ)!

I pray your angels will know him well, Lord. Not for the messes they've yanked him out of, but because of his love for you.

You have "gone into heaven" and are "at God's right hand— with angels, authorities and powers in submission" to you (1 Peter 3:22).

Please watch over my child wherever he goes.

a ESV, b NLT, c NLT, d ESV, e ESV

WALKING THE
WATERS OF WORRY

Then Peter got down out of the boat,
walked on the water and came toward
Jesus. But when he saw the wind, he
was afraid and, beginning to sink, cried
out, "Lord, save me!" Immediately Jesus
reached out his hand and caught him.
"You of little faith," he said, "why did you
doubt?"

Matthew 14:29–31

I think I would have done the same thing Peter did, Lord.

As long as he had his eyes on you, everything was fine.

But it didn't take much for him to be distracted—just "the wind" (Matthew 14:30)! And as soon as he started worrying about it, "Peter (which means 'rock')" (Matthew 16:18[a]) sank like a stone.

I have walked in his footsteps—but not on water.

Even though you tell us, "Do not worry about tomorrow" (Matthew 6:34[b]), sometimes it's very difficult for me not to do that—especially as a parent!

But you were right there for Peter. "Immediately" you "reached out" your hand and "caught him" (Matthew 14:31)—you didn't let him sink too far!

Thank you that we can come to you with our worries, Lord! Your Word teaches me to "give all" my "worries and cares" to you, because you genuinely care for us (1 Peter 5:7ᶜ). Peter himself wrote that!

You have everything I need in your hands. But I need you most of all.

Through your power to answer prayer you can change the most challenging circumstances for the better, and bring good out of them that I never thought was possible.

I pray that my child will learn this and know the peace that you give, Lord Jesus.

When, like Martha, she is "worried and upset about many things" (Luke 10:41), I pray that you will help her find "what is better" (Luke 10:42)—time spent at your feet.

I know I'm asking for something my child and I both need, but I also know it's something you love to give. That's why it was prophesied about you, "He will be our peace" (Micah 5:5).

You are my peace, Lord Jesus! And I pray that you will be my child's as well. Please give us both more of your Spirit so that we will live in your peace more and more.

I pray that you will "increase our faith" (Luke 17:5ᵈ) so that when difficulties come we will trust you to be as faithful in the future as you have been in the past.

You promised in your Word, "I the Lord do not change" (Malachi 3:6). The same faithfulness you have always had for your people you will also have for us!

"Sovereign LORD, you are God! Your covenant is trustworthy" (2 Samuel 7:28). "You faithfully answer our prayers with awesome deeds, O God our savior" (Psalm 65:5e).

Peter called out, "Lord, save me!" (Matthew 14:30) and you reached out your hand and pulled him up.

Save us from the 'waters of worry,' Lord, and draw us close!

I praise you that now, just as then, your arm "is not too short to save" (Isaiah 59:1)!

STORMS

"There is no one like the God of Israel.
He rides across the heavens to help you,
across the skies in majestic splendor."

Deuteronomy 33:26 (NLT)

Storms can be scary, Lord.

There's so much power in them, and they can make us feel so small.

I think of the times when thunder rolled and my child would jump out of his bed into mine. He wanted to get close enough to hear my heart beat, just to feel safe.

I'm also reminded of the time you "rebuked the wind and said to the waves, 'Quiet! Be still!' Then the wind died down and it was completely calm" (Mark 4:39). The disciples "were terrified and asked each other, "Who is this? Even the wind and the waves obey him!" (Mark 4:41).

Your power amazes me too, Lord, but so does your heart!

You are "the Lord Almighty" (1 Samuel 4:4) who "makes the clouds his chariot and rides on the wings of the wind" (Psalm 104:3).

But you also ride "across the heavens to help" us (Deuteronomy 33:26[a])! You are "the compassionate and gracious God, slow to anger, abounding in love and faithfulness, maintaining love to thousands, and forgiving wickedness, rebellion and sin (Exodus 34:6–7).

I praise you, Jesus, because you are Lord over every storm that will ever occur in my child's life. Please watch over him and keep him safe.

Please speak to the storms when they rage and he is frightened, but also speak to his heart. You are able to calm the storms within, and when they come, I pray he will hear your voice saying, "Peace, be still" (Mark 4:39[b]).

When life's troubles raged around David, he wrote, "Oh, that I had the wings of a dove! I would fly away and be at rest. . . . I would hurry to my place of shelter, far from the tempest and storm" (Psalm 55:6, 8).

I pray you will be my son's shelter too Lord! May he always "take refuge in the shelter of your wings" (Psalm 61:4).

What is a storm to you? "The billowing clouds are" simply "the dust beneath" your "feet" (Nahum 1:3[c]).

I praise you that my son will never encounter a difficulty that you cannot handle.

There is no storm that could ever be a match for you. Nothing is stronger than you, Lord, and there is "no one greater" (Hebrews 6:13)!

I pray that my son will always know this: your "name" is "a strong tower; the righteous man runs into it and is safe" (Proverbs 18:10[d]).

"When the storms of life come, the wicked are whirled away, but the godly have a lasting foundation" (Proverbs 10:25^e).

May he always have a firm and safe foundation for his life, Lord Jesus, because you are his "cornerstone" (Ephesians 2:20^f).

a NLT, b NKJV, c NLT, d ESV, e NLT, f ESV

UP WORDS

Why am I discouraged? Why is my heart
so sad?
I will put my hope in God! I will praise him
again—
my Savior and my God!

Psalm 43:5 (NLT)

Sometimes my child feels low, and my heart goes out to him.

How I wish I could reach inside and lift him up!

But only you can do that, Lord. You can touch his heart, and "put a new song" in his mouth, "a song of praise" to you (Psalm 40:3ᵃ)!

I do not ask you that his life will always be easy. Difficult times can teach us much!

I understand that sometimes "suffering" is "good" for us, because it teaches us "to pay attention" (Psalm 119:71ᵇ) to you and what you want for our lives.

You wrote the 'owner's manual'! And your Word shows us the direction to take when we are down: "Why am I discouraged? Why is my heart so sad? I will put my hope" in you! "I will praise" you again—"my Savior and my God!" (Psalm 43:5^c).

Father, I pray that you will help my child to learn to do what David did. When he was "greatly distressed" and the people around him were "bitter in soul," David "strengthened himself" in you, "his God" (1 Samuel 30:6^d).

I pray that my child will run to you when it feels like the world is crumbling around him.

One day, "the earth will wear out like a garment," but your "salvation will last forever," and your "righteousness will never fail" (Isaiah 51:6).

When my child asks, "where does my help come from?", may his heart be quick to answer, "My help comes from the LORD, the Maker of heaven and earth" (Psalm 121:1–2).

Please teach him to praise you, Father! Turn his eyes to you and help him to learn to say, "Though I sit in darkness, the LORD will be my light" (Micah 7:8^e).

"Light shines upon the righteous and joy on the upright in heart" (Psalm 97:11). When the world around him is dark, I pray he will turn to your light and follow you into fresh new places of praise!

The more we learn to take our minds off our problems and place them on you, the more we are blessed. "The cheerful of heart has a continual feast" (Proverbs 15:15^f), so I pray you will help him to learn to feast on all that you are!

Like Joshua, may he sense your Spirit telling him, "Do not be discouraged, for the LORD your God will be with you wherever you go" (Joshua 1:9).

A man who needed you was told once, "Cheer up . . . He's calling you!" (Mark 10:49).

I pray that my son will hear your voice and that you will "encourage" his heart and "strengthen" him "in every good deed and word" (2 Thessalonians 2:17).

Please lift him up, Lord, and hold him close to your heart. You are "close to the brokenhearted," and you save "those who are crushed in spirit" (Psalm 34:18). You give us "eternal encouragement and good hope" (2 Thessalonians 2:16)!

I pray my son will be eternally encouraged in you! Even though we "may have many troubles" in this life, you are greater still. And in the end, you will deliver us "from them all" (Psalm 34:19).

a ESV, b NLT, c NLT, d ESV, e NLT, f ESV

SLEEPING BEAUTY

My help comes from the LORD, the Maker
of heaven and earth.
He will not let your foot slip—he who
watches over you will not slumber;
indeed, he who watches over Israel will
neither slumber nor sleep.

Psalm 121:2–4

There are few things more beautiful than a sleeping child. How I loved to watch her sleep, Father!

Sometimes I would stand there the longest time, rapt with wonder at the miracle you had blessed us with, thinking of all she would be.

Do you look on us in the same way, Father?

You "decided in advance to adopt us" as your children (Ephesians 1:5ᵃ) through your precious Son.

Your desire is for us to be "blameless and pure," shining "like stars in the sky" (Philippians 2:15).

You stand there watching "over" us and "neither slumber nor sleep" (Psalm 121:4), gazing on us with a deeper love than we could ever comprehend.

You love us so much that you, "the everlasting God" (Isaiah 40:28ᵇ), went to the grave and back to bring us home to yourself.

You even said that your people are your "most precious possession" (Zechariah 2:8ᶜ)! And thinking about that makes me wonder all the more. . . .

When you look on my sleeping child, what is it you see?

"No one can fathom" your "understanding" (Isaiah 40:28). You see strength and grace yet to be awakened within her that no one else sees!

Lord Jesus, I praise you because even though you love us where we are, you do not leave us there. When we receive you, you save us from our sins and help us to grow. We even "become heirs having the hope of eternal life" (Titus 3:7).

You not only treasure my child as she is, you see what she will one day be!

You said that one day "the righteous will shine like the sun in the kingdom of their Father" (Matthew 13:43ᵈ). You can already see her there, standing in "the holy city, the New Jerusalem" (Revelation 21:2), shining brightly in the salvation you have secured for us.

But before she gets there, she must grow in the grace that "teaches us to say 'No' to ungodliness and worldly passions, and to live self-controlled, upright and godly lives in this present age, while we wait for the blessed hope"—your "appearing," our "great God and Savior" (Titus 2:12–13)!

Isn't that why your Word also tells us to "wake up," because "our salvation is nearer now than when we first believed" (Romans 13:11ᵉ)?

We are only becoming aware of all that you are and all that you are calling us to be!

So your Spirit tells us, "Awake, O sleeper, and arise from the dead, and Christ will shine on you" (Ephesians 5:14[f]).

"Let the light of your face shine" upon her, Lord (Psalm 4:6), and awaken your hope within.

May your every dream for my child come true. Then she will "walk in the light of your presence" (Psalm 89:15) forever!

a NLT, b ESV, c NLT, d ESV, e NLT, f ESV

READY . . . OR NOT

"So you also must be ready, because the
Son of Man will come at an hour when
you do not expect him."

Matthew 24:44

Sometimes when we would play games as children we would say, 'Ready or not, here I come!'

Please get him ready, Lord Jesus.

Ready for what really matters.

Ready for "the day of" your return (Joel 2:1).

You talked about it often, telling us to "be ready" because you will come when we "do not expect" you (Matthew 24:44).

And you're not playing games.

Your Word is very clear on that. It tells us that day "will come like a thief. The heavens will disappear with a roar; the elements will be destroyed by fire, and the earth and everything in it will be laid bare" (2 Peter 3:10).

Oh, Lord! What a day that will be! "While people are saying, 'There is peace and security,' then sudden destruction will come" (1 Thessalonians 5:3[a]).

Because we "do not know" when you "will come," I pray that you will help both me and my child to "keep watch" (Matthew 24:42).

May even the clouds remind us, because you said "in days to come" we "will see the Son of Man sitting at the right hand of the Mighty One and coming on the clouds of heaven" (Matthew 26:64[b]).

Thank you that we don't have to "be surprised when the day" comes (1 Thessalonians 5:4[c]); we can even look forward to it!

When you "appear a second time," you will "save those who are eagerly waiting" for you (Hebrews 9:28[d])!

Father, I praise you because you "chose to save us through our Lord Jesus Christ, not to pour out" your "anger on us" (1 Thessalonians 5:9[e]).

"He died for us" so that we "may live together with him" (1 Thessalonians 5:10)!

I pray that you will help my child always to be aware of your presence, Lord, and to "stay alert and be clearheaded" (1 Thessalonians 5:6[f]).

Help him to "be careful" so that his heart will not be "weighed down with carousing, drunkenness and the anxieties of life" (Luke 21:34). Let his heart be lifted up with the hope of being with you!

May the cry of his heart be, "I look to the LORD for help. I wait confidently for God to save me, and my God will certainly hear me" (Micah 7:7[g]).

I pray that my child will "long for" you (Psalm 130:6[h]), Lord Jesus!

You said that "no one can come" to you "unless the Father who sent" you "draws them" to you (John 6:44[i]). Please draw him near, Father!

Then, even while he lives on this earth he will be among the "citizens of heaven," and will be "eagerly waiting" for your Son "to return as our Savior" (Philippians 3:20[j]).

a ESV, b NIrV, c NLT, d ESV, e NLT, f NLT, g NLT, h NLT, i NLT, j NLT

Week 12

OVERCOMING

Love When We're over Our Heads

> "Daddy . . . who was praying for me Tuesday night?"
>
> Chrissy Cymbala Toledo[8]

"God will never allow you to go through more than you can bear."

You hear people say it all the time, and they mean it kindly. It's something you hear when you're in a hard place, and it's intended as a reminder of God's faithfulness. But comforting as those words are, there's a problem with them.

God never made that promise.

Here's what His Word actually says: "No temptation has overtaken you except what is common to mankind. And God is faithful; *he will not let you be tempted beyond what you can bear.* But when you are tempted, he will also provide a way out so that you can endure it" (1 Corinthians 10:13, italics added).

---

8. As quoted by Jim Cymbala in *Fresh Wind, Fresh Fire*, p. 113.

It may be the most misquoted verse in Scripture—and the difference between the two thoughts shouldn't be missed. God promises us a way out when we face temptation, but it's not a generality applied to all of life's problems. When we think that, we set ourselves up for a painful misunderstanding. What do you do in those crushing moments when life's circumstances are more than you can bear? Where do you turn? Do you give up on God and decide that He is no longer faithful? Do you stop praying because it "didn't work," or think that God has given up on you?

The hard truth is that life sometimes is more than we can bear. But we were never intended to bear it alone. God *has* promised, "Never will I leave you, never will I forsake you" (Hebrews 13:5). Jesus said, "I am with you *always*" (Matthew 28:20, italics added). But that doesn't mean that life's circumstances won't sometimes drive us to our knees. And it's there that we're in the best position for God to help us.

We can be tempted to believe that "God helps those who help themselves"—but that isn't in the Bible either. God isn't into "self-reliance." He's into dependence. Jesus said of His relationship to the Father, "By myself I can do nothing" (John 5:30). He also said, "Apart from me, *you* can do nothing" (John 15:5, italics added). It's often in the middle of our problems that a tough but comforting truth comes to meet us. When God allows us to go through more than we can bear, we discover the depth of our need for Him. When we come to the end of ourselves, we find that He is enough.

The apostle John, who as the disciple who outlived all the others was no stranger to heartache, wrote that "everyone born of God overcomes the world." Then he added,

"This is the victory that has overcome the world, *even our faith*" (1 John 5:4, italics added). God has a way of showing himself faithful when we're in over our heads. Not the faithfulness of saving us from our circumstances, though He sometimes does that, but the faithfulness of meeting us in unexpected places and pouring new strength into us. As we wait for Him and turn to Him, He lifts us out of our self-focus—the thought that our own lives are the center of the universe—and carries us to new places of praise. That's why David would write in the middle of an unresolved difficulty, "Praise the LORD; praise God our Savior! For each day He carries us in His arms" (Psalm 68:19 NLT).

Jesus said, "In this world you will have trouble. But take heart! I have overcome the world" (John 16:33). This week we'll pray that our children will also, through Him. We'll ask that they may persevere in faith with "strength of character" and "confident hope of salvation" (Romans 5:3–4 NLT) because they "know whom" they "have believed" (2 Timothy 1:12).

These are prayers that take the long view, seeing our children through life's adversity and all the way home.

SOMEONE WITH HIM . . . IN THE FIRE

> Then King Nebuchadnezzar leaped to
> his feet in amazement and asked his
> advisers,
> "Weren't there three men that we tied up
> and threw into the fire?"
> They replied, "Certainly, Your Majesty." He
> said, "Look! I see four men
> walking around in the fire, unbound and
> unharmed,
> and the fourth looks like a son of the
> gods."
>
> Daniel 3:24–25

I know there will be days when my son will have to walk through the fire, Lord.

Your Word tells us that difficulties are part of life; we are "born to trouble as surely as sparks fly upward" (Job 5:7). I wish I could keep him from it, but I also understand that he will find strength in the fire that can be forged nowhere else: "suffering produces perseverance; perseverance,

279 • Someone with Him . . . in the Fire

character; and character, hope. And hope does not put us to shame," because you have "poured out" your love "into our hearts through the Holy Spirit, who has been given to us" (Romans 5:3–5).

My prayer today is not he will have a trouble-free life, but that you will be with him when he walks through the fire.

You, the God who does not change, have promised your people your presence in the most challenging circumstances of life. You told us, "When you pass through the waters, I will be with you; and through the rivers, they shall not overwhelm you; when you walk through fire you shall not be burned, and the flame shall not consume you. For I am the LORD your God, the Holy One of Israel, your Savior" (Isaiah 43:2–3[a]).

I praise you, Lord Jesus, that as Almighty God you are "the same yesterday and today and forever" (Hebrews 13:8[b]), and your promises can be trusted.

When Nebuchadnezzar had Shadrach, Meshach, and Abednego thrown into the fire and "there were four men walking around," and "the fourth" looked like "a son of the gods" (Daniel 3:24–25), you were with them, weren't you?

Haven't you told us, "I am with you always, even to the end of the age" (Matthew 28:20[c])?

When my child walks through the fire, Lord, I pray that you will be with him too, and that he will be "unbound and unharmed" (Daniel 3:25). May he only go through that which you in your perfect wisdom know is necessary for his character and hope to grow.

When there is the smoke of confusion around him, may his relationship with you give him all the direction he needs. I pray that his "own ears will hear" you guiding him. "Right behind" him "a voice will say, 'This is the way you should go,' whether to the right or to the left" (Isaiah 30:21[d]).

Your Word says, "A friend loves at all times, and a brother is born for adversity" (Proverbs 17:17[e]). There is no friend like you!

Your Word also says, "There is a friend who sticks closer than a brother" (Proverbs 18:24[f]). You are that friend— no one sticks closer than you.

You are Immanuel, "God with us" (Matthew 1:23)!

And I praise you for being with my son wherever he goes.

a ESV, b ESV, c NKJV, d NLT, e ESV, f ESV

WHEN A LAMB
WIPES TEARS AWAY

To all who mourn in Israel, he will give a
    crown of beauty for ashes,
a joyous blessing instead of mourning, fes-
    tive praise instead of despair.
In their righteousness, they will be like
    great oaks
that the LORD has planted for his own glory.

Isaiah 61:3 (NLT)

My child's tears have always touched my heart, Lord.

But I'm moved by the fact that they touch yours even more. Your Word says that "you keep track" of all our sorrows. "You have collected" all our "tears in your bottle. You have recorded each one in your book" (Psalm 56:8[a]).

Nothing escapes you, Father! Not even the slightest sigh.

I praise you and thank you for your tender love. "How kind" you are! "How good" you are! "So merciful" (Psalm 116:5[b])!

Today I pray that my child will know the comfort you can give her heart. You are even able to tell us that when we mourn, we're "blessed" (Matthew 5:4ᶜ)—blessed because there is a comfort only you can give.

You can always be trusted to keep your promises. How you love your people, Lord!

I love the promise in your Word that you will one day "wipe every tear" from our eyes. "There will be no more death or sorrow or crying or pain." All of these things will be "gone forever" (Revelation 21:4ᵈ)!

You, "the Lamb on the throne," will be our "Shepherd," and you will lead us to "springs of life-giving water" (Revelation 7:17ᵉ).

I wish I could always be there to wipe my child's tears away, but I know there will be tears my hands can't touch.

So I place her in your hands today, and thank you for your perfect compassion and love. You are "the Lamb of God, who takes away the sin of the world!" (John 1:29ᶠ).

Beautiful Savior, you are so gentle with us.

You do "not treat us as our sins deserve or repay us according to our iniquities" (Psalm 103:10).

You were "pierced for our transgressions," and "crushed for our iniquities; the punishment that brought us peace was upon" you, and by your "wounds we are healed" (Isaiah 53:5).

You "wept over" your people (Luke 19:41ᵍ) wanting them to know your peace, and you went to the cross so that our own tears may one day be no more.

By faith I see my child there, standing before you on that day. A "crown of beauty" (Isaiah 61:3ʰ) rests where time and care once drew their lines.

How she has grown! "Perseverance" has finished "its work" so that she is "mature and complete, not lacking anything" (James 1:4).

Your hand touches her face and in a single motion every sorrow is swept away and only your peace remains.

This is my prayer for my daughter, Lord. May she be among "those the LORD has rescued" who return and "enter Zion with singing." And may she stand in wonder before you, as she is welcomed into the "everlasting joy" (Isaiah 35:10) of your amazing love.

WORLD'S WORST BULLY

Then there was war in heaven. Michael
and his angels fought
against the dragon and his angels. And
the dragon lost the battle,
and he and his angels were forced out of
heaven. This great dragon—
the ancient serpent called the devil,
or Satan, the one deceiving the whole
world—was thrown down to the earth with
all his angels.

Revelation 12:7–9 (NLT)

I can hardly wait for you to deal with the devil once and for all, Lord.

He has caused so much pain and heartache in this world. But when your kingdom comes that will all be behind us!

One day you have promised to create "a new heaven and a new earth, where righteousness dwells"—and I am "looking forward" to it (2 Peter 3:13)!

But until then, the world's worst bully is still on the prowl. "He is filled with fury, because he knows that his time is short" (Revelation 12:12)—and I pray that you will protect my child from him.

I praise you, Lord, that because of what you did at the cross we face a defeated foe.

You "disarmed the spiritual rulers and authorities," and "shamed them publicly" by your "victory over them on the cross" (Colossians 2:15[a]).

So even though our adversary has power, he has no authority. "All authority in heaven and on earth has been given" to you, Lord Jesus (Matthew 28:18[b])!

Through your amazing power and mercy, you have even given us authority "to overcome all the power of the enemy" (Luke 10:19).

Even though there are still battles to fight, the war is won! And those who receive you can "rejoice" that their "names are written in heaven" (Luke 10:20[c]).

I pray that my son will have a healthy, humble understanding of all you have done so that he may live in obedience to you and not be defeated or afraid when the enemy tries to tempt or attack him.

May he understand that his strength to overcome the evil one is only found in you. May he be among those who "listen to" your voice and "follow" you, Lord Jesus (John 10:27[d]). You have promised that "they will never perish, and no one will snatch them" out of your hand (John 10:28[e]).

Thank you for watching over him day and night. You are always vigilant! You neither "slumber nor sleep" (Psalm 121:4[f]).

Please help him to vigilant as well. I pray that he will be "alert and of sober mind" (1 Peter 5:8), so that he will "not be outwitted by Satan" or "ignorant of" his many schemes (2 Corinthians 2:11[g]).

May my son also know you are always watching, and may that thought encourage him and keep him from sinning. Your eyes "search the whole earth in order to strengthen those whose hearts are fully committed" to you (2 Chronicles 16:9[h]).

I praise you, Lord Jesus, because the devil is no match for you. You "saw Satan fall like lightning from heaven" (Luke 10:18[i]).

I pray that my child will "resist the devil" and that the devil "will flee" from him (James 4:7). And "may your Kingdom come soon" (Matthew 6:10[j]), so that every battle is won!

a NLT, b ESV, c ESV, d NLT, e ESV, f ESV, g ESV, h NLT, i ESV, j NLT

JUMPING FOR JOY

He will keep you firm to the end, so that you will be blameless on the day of our Lord Jesus Christ. God is faithful, who has called you into fellowship with his Son, Jesus Christ our Lord.

1 Corinthians 1:8–9

It can be a scary thing raising children in this world, Lord.

I think about how precious my child is and how I would do anything I could to protect her!

But more than anything else, I want her to be a faithful believer. I know there is no greater protection for her than to rest secure "in the shadow of your wings" (Psalm 36:7ᵃ).

Father, when I think what it must have been like for you to see your Son voluntarily suffer for our sins, my own heart as a parent is moved with compassion.

I cannot imagine what you went through! I am so sorry and so thankful—because I know you did it to rescue me from my sins.

And after you rescue us, you're right there with us! You even promise to "keep" us "strong to the very end" (1 Corinthians 1:8[b])!

So today I pray that my child will know the strength that only you can give.

Father, your Word makes it clear that "all who desire to live a godly life in Christ Jesus will be persecuted, while evil people and impostors will go on from bad to worse" (2 Timothy 3:12–13[c]).

These are evil times we live in, and I understand that because my child believes in you, life will not always be easy for her. You alone know what she will have to face, but I want to thank you in advance for being there for her. You have "called" her into a relationship with your Son, and you are "faithful" (1 Corinthians 1:9)!

Lord Jesus, it hurts to think that my child will face difficulty because of her faith, but I praise you because you have everything under control. As she stays close to you, I know that all will be well.

As we walk with you through difficulty, you make us more like you. We are "transformed into" your "image with ever-increasing glory" through the strength of your Spirit (2 Corinthians 3:18).

You even said, "Blessed are you when people insult you, persecute you and falsely say all kinds of evil against you because of me. Rejoice and be glad, because great is your reward in heaven" (Matthew 5:11–12). You not only said to "rejoice in that day," you also told us to "leap for joy" (Luke 6:23[d]) because the heavenly reward will be so great!

So I pray you will give her grace in that moment to see beyond sorrow—and make the leap of faith into the joy and peace of your presence.

You, "for the joy set before" you, "endured the cross, scorning its shame, and sat down at the right hand of the throne of God" (Hebrews 12:2).

I thank you for where the road comes out, Lord. As my daughter takes up her "cross" to "follow" you (Matthew 10:38[e]), the joy of all you are will be her best reward.

Then she will sit smiling at your feet forever.

a ESV, b NIrV, c ESV, d ESV, e ESV

THE CROSS AND THE FIGHT

I have fought the good fight,
I have finished the race,
I have kept the faith.

2 Timothy 4:7

I pray that my child will really follow you, Lord Jesus. But that isn't easy.

You said, "If anyone would come after me, let him deny himself and take up his cross daily and follow me" (Luke 9:23ᵃ).

You also said that if we "refuse to take up" our crosses and follow you, we "are not worthy" of being yours (Matthew 10:38ᵇ).

We can only live for you if you give us strength. Our faith must "rest on" your "power" (1 Corinthians 2:5) and nothing less!

But we must give you nothing less than our best.

I'm reminded of what the apostle Paul wrote near the end of his life: "I have fought the good fight, I have finished the race" (2 Timothy 4:7).

He tried, hard! He didn't say, 'What a walk in the park!'

Paul fought and he ran. He said he ran "with purpose in every step," and he wasn't "just shadowboxing" (1 Corinthians 9:26[c]).

I praise you that you can help my child overcome every obstacle he faces, including his own will! Please give him the strength to surrender himself to you every day.

You didn't live for yourself on this earth. You said that you came "down from heaven, not to do" your "own will but the will of him who sent" you (John 6:38[d]).

I pray that my child will live for your will as well, Lord. Please help him not to live for what he wants, but for what you want.

Help him to understand that if we "cling to" our lives we "will lose" them, but if we "give up" our lives for you, we "will find" them (Matthew 10:39[e]).

I pray that you will help him to understand that we were made for you, and our lives are without lasting purpose apart from you.

You said, "As the Father has sent me, so I am sending you" (John 20:21[f]). Please help my child to understand that there is so much more to live for than our own plans and pleasures.

You surpass them all! There is nothing better than knowing you.

So I ask that you will help my child to "throw off everything that hinders and the sin that so easily entangles" and "run with perseverance the race marked out for" him (Hebrews 12:1).

I pray that he will have "patient endurance" to go the distance so that he "will continue to do" your will. Then he "will receive all" that you have "promised" (Hebrews 10:36^g)!

May he run to you, "Jesus, the pioneer and perfecter of faith" (Hebrews 12:2)!

May his "soul live and praise you" (Psalm 119:175[h]), because "neither death nor life, neither angels nor demons, neither our fears for today nor our worries about tomorrow—not even the powers of hell can separate us" from your love. "No power in the sky above or in the earth below . . . nothing in all creation will ever be able to separate us" from your love (Romans 8:38–39[i])!

I thank you that the fight can be won, the race finished and the faith kept, because your "faithful love endures forever" (2 Chronicles 20:21[j])!

a NLT, b ESV, c ESV, d NLT, e ESV, f ESV, g ESV, h NLT, i ESV, j NLT

DELIVERED

I prayed to the LORD, and he answered me.
He freed me from all my fears.
Those who look to him for help will be radiant with joy; no shadow of shame
will darken their faces. In my desperation I
prayed, and the LORD listened;
he saved me from all my troubles.

Psalm 34:4–6 (NLT)

How many times have you helped me in my life, Lord?

You have "delivered" me "from trouble" (Proverbs 11:8[a]) again and again!

You are my "refuge and strength, an ever-present help in trouble" (Psalm 46:1)! And I praise you because you are more than able to help my child as well.

I pray that my son will call on you whenever he is in trouble, Father. Isn't that what your Word tells us to do? "Are any of you in trouble? Then you should pray" (James 5:13[b]).

Even when we are surrounded on all sides, the way up is always open. You are the "one who breaks open the way" (Micah 2:13)!

How blessed we are to be able to call on you in prayer. You are "near to all who call" on you, "to all who call" on you honestly and from the heart (Psalm 145:18ᶜ). You fulfill "the desires of those who fear" you. You hear "their cry" and save them, because you watch "over all who love" you (Psalm 145:19–20).

Even when we don't see trouble coming we can still trust you to help us. You tell us that "the godly may trip seven times, but they will get up again" (Proverbs 24:16ᵈ). We rise because you lift us up.

"As soon as" we pray, "you answer" us; "you encourage" us "by giving" us "strength" (Psalm 138:3ᵉ)—because you yourself are the best answer to prayer.

Even when our circumstances do not seem to change, we can trust that your transforming power is at work. "For you bless the godly, O LORD; you surround them with your shield of love" (Psalm 5:12ᶠ). Just being in your presence "turns" our "darkness into light" (2 Samuel 22:29). You are the "the Awesome One" (Psalm 76:11ᵍ)!

"Great" is your "faithfulness," Lord! Your "mercies begin afresh each morning" (Lamentations 3:23ʰ). Let each "morning bring" him "word of your unfailing love" because he puts his "trust in you" (Psalm 143:8).

When we are "overwhelmed, you alone know the way" we "should turn" (Psalm 142:3ⁱ).

Whenever my child is in trouble I pray he will "look to you for protection" and "hide beneath the shadow of your wings until the danger passes by" (Psalm 57:1ʲ).

Please "show" him your "unfailing love and faithfulness," Lord (2 Samuel 15:20ᵏ).

You have "rescued us from the dominion of darkness and brought us into the kingdom of the Son" you love, "in whom we have redemption, the forgiveness of sins" (Colossians 1:13–14).

May the strong cry of my son's heart be, "The Lord will deliver me from every evil attack and will bring me safely into his heavenly Kingdom. All glory to God forever and ever! Amen" (2 Timothy 4:18[l])!

a ESV, b NIrV, c ESV, d NLT, e NLT, f NLT, g NLT, h NLT, i NLT, j NLT, k NLT, l NLT

"COME TO THE TABLE!"

"People will come from east and west and
north and south, and will take their places
at the feast in the kingdom of God."

Luke 13:29

I can see my child at that banquet, Lord.

There she is! She looks beautiful, "dressed in white" (Revelation 3:4), not a single line or care on her face.

She has come to "sit down with Abraham, Isaac, and Jacob at the feast in the Kingdom of Heaven" (Matthew 8:11[a]).

So many others are there too! There's the "Roman officer" (Matthew 8:5[b]) whose faith impressed you so much, and there's "Lazarus" seated close to Abraham (Luke 16:23[c]). He was poor and disregarded on this earth, but he's in a place of honor now.

I can only imagine the conversation around that table. What incredible stories we will hear of your amazing faithfulness, made all the more clear once our "race" is run (2 Timothy 4:7) and we "know fully" (1 Corinthians 13:12[d]) all that you have done for us.

We will have our stories too, and in each of them we "will give glory to your name forever" (Psalm 86:12ᵉ)!

Oh, Lord, I so look forward to being there! And I pray that all of our family will be.

I pray that my child will "make every effort to enter through the narrow door" (Luke 13:24) that leads to the kingdom of heaven. You are "the door," Lord Jesus. "If anyone enters" by you, that person "will be saved" (John 10:9ᶠ).

"We are looking forward to a new heaven and a new earth, where righteousness dwells" (2 Peter 3:13), promised to all who repent of their sins and turn to you.

One day in the "new Jerusalem" (Revelation 3:12ᵍ) you "will spread a wonderful feast." You "will remove the cloud of gloom, the shadow of death that hangs over the earth," and "will wipe away all tears" (Isaiah 25:6–8ʰ).

What a day that will be! "In that day" we will proclaim, "This is our God! We trusted" in you, and you "saved us!" We will always "rejoice in the salvation" you give (Isaiah 25:9ⁱ)—an adventure in unlimited life and love with you that never ends!

"People will come from east and west and north and south" (Luke 13:29) and we will praise you with a shout, "Salvation belongs to our God who sits on the throne, and to the Lamb!" (Revelation 7:10ʲ).

I'm reminded of what John heard an angel say: "Blessed are those who are invited to the wedding supper of the Lamb!" (Revelation 19:9).

May my child come to that table, Lord Jesus!

I pray she will know how much you love her—and be filled with so much love for you—that she may sing for joy, "He has brought me to his banqueting hall, and his banner over me is love" (Song of Songs 2:4[k]).

a NLT, b NLT, c ESV, d ESV, e NLT, f ESV, g ESV, h NLT, i NLT, j ESV, k NASB

Week 13

BLESSED

"It Just Keeps Getting Better"

> Let none of us be content . . . until [Jesus]
> has received our children, and has so
> blessed them that we are sure that they
> have entered the Kingdom of God.
>
> Charles Haddon Spurgeon

"Say good-bye to a good night's sleep!"

"There goes your freedom!"

"Just you wait! Your life is really going to change."

When our baby girl was born, we heard all kinds of opinions. One stood head and shoulders above the rest.

It belonged to Mal King, an FBI-trained criminal investigator who also had daughters. One day I shared with him some little thing my three month old had done. He smiled broadly and said, "It just keeps getting better."

Mal was more than an optimist. He had seen a lot of life and could have viewed things very differently. But he trusted God deeply—and that confidence hung in the air with his words. His was a statement of faith I would never forget.

"It just keeps getting better." Learn to rest in God, and you have something to look forward to, no matter what life may hold. A blessed life can't be measured by possessions or health or a few short years when things go well on this earth. When you're truly blessed, eternity opens wide before you with a hope—the very presence of the living Lord Jesus—that presses in on the moment. "Christ in you, the hope of glory" (Colossians 1:27), is how the apostle Paul described it. And when our sons and daughters take Jesus to heart, they live large in the big life that only God can give them—"life by the power of his name" (John 20:31 NLT).

The prayers in these last pages are written so that our children may be blessed with the "all-surpassing" life God gives (2 Corinthians 4:7) and finish well. You'll find prayers for their relationships with God and others, for purpose and direction in life, and for their eternal destiny. As you pray, I hope you'll keep in mind the moments when Jesus "took the children in his arms, placed his hands on them and blessed them" (Mark 10:16). Whatever your children's ages, imagine bringing them to Jesus so He may touch them and "they may take hold of the life that is truly life" (1 Timothy 6:19).

We can think of so many ways we want our children to be blessed, but Jesus knows how to bless them best for an eternal lifetime. Heaven has been described as "the Great Story which no one on earth has read: which goes on for ever: in which every chapter is better than the one before." These are prayers that the hope of heaven will shine into our children's souls even now, and be the story of their lives forever.

FOREVER BLESSED

He said to them, "Let the little children
come to me, and do not hinder them,
for the kingdom of God belongs to such
as these. Truly I tell you, anyone who will
not receive the kingdom of God like a
little child will never enter it." And he took
the children in his arms, placed his hands
on them and blessed them.

Mark 10:14–16

I can see my son in that verse, Lord.

There he is, standing right in front of you. You have both hands on his shoulders, and you are smiling . . . looking in his eyes and blessing him.

What more could my child possibly need than your blessing and favor? So by faith I bring him to you through this prayer and ask that you bless him.

I never want to do anything to "hinder" him from coming to you (Matthew 19:14)! Where I have "hidden faults" (Psalm 19:12[a]) I'm not even aware of, don't let them interfere with his coming to you.

"I am your servant; give me discernment that I may understand" (Psalm 119:125) what you want me to do to help him know and love you.

"You are the God of great wonders! You demonstrate your awesome power" (Psalm 77:14[b]) in amazing ways!

You have even hidden spiritual truths "from the wise and learned, and revealed them to little children" (Luke 10:21).

I ask that my son will receive you and "the Kingdom of God like a child" (Luke 18:17[c]), so that he may enjoy you forever.

Just as he once ran to me whenever he had a need, I pray he will learn to "run to you" (Isaiah 55:5[d]), depending on you moment by moment.

May he hear your "still small voice" (1 Kings 19:12[e]) speaking to him about all that you are, convicting him of his sin and leading him "into all truth" (John 16:13[f]), closer and closer to you.

It is human nature to follow our own wisdom. "All of us, like sheep, have strayed away. We have left" your paths "to follow our own" (Isaiah 53:6[g]).

We are lost without you!

But with you, we are "washed," "sanctified," and "justified in the name of the Lord Jesus Christ and by the Spirit of our God" (1 Corinthians 6:11[h]).

So here is my child, Lord. I bring him before you today.

I pray that you will bless him, Lord. Bless him as you know best!

Please touch him and bless him in whatever ways he needs most, so that there may be no doubt that your "hand" is "with" him (Acts 11:21).

May your hand be with him wherever he goes! May he know the peace of your presence in his soul and live every day in a close and lasting friendship with you.

Please keep blessing my child beyond my years, until we stop counting the years and they are no more.

"When you grant a blessing, O Lord, it is an eternal blessing!" (1 Chronicles 17:27[i]).

I pray that my child may be forever blessed!

a ESV, b NLT, c NLT, d NKJV, e NKJV, f NLT, g NLT, h ESV, i NLT

WHAT TO WEAR

Therefore, as God's chosen people, holy
and dearly loved, clothe yourselves with
compassion, kindness, humility, gentleness
and patience.

Colossians 3:12

'I don't have anything to wear!'

How many times have you heard us say that, Father, even
though we have clothing to spare?

I pray my child will wear what you want her to, Lord. But
that's about so much more than clothes!

You want us to "walk as children of light" (Ephesians 5:8ᵃ),
and "clothe" ourselves "with compassion, kindness,
humility, gentleness and patience" (Colossians 3:12).

You are "a God of compassion and mercy, slow to get angry
and filled with unfailing love and faithfulness" (Psalm
86:15ᵇ).

"O LORD my God, how great you are! You are robed with
honor and majesty. You are dressed in a robe of light"
(Psalm 104:1–2ᶜ).

You want others to see you in us! So I ask that my child will be dressed in the beauty of your "love and mercy" (Isaiah 63:9).

I pray she will "have compassion" on those in need (Matthew 15:32[d]) as you do, Lord Jesus, and that she will act with kindness in ways that point others to your presence in her life.

Your Word tells us to "sympathize with each other," to "love each other as brothers and sisters," to "be tenderhearted," and to "keep a humble attitude" (1 Peter 3:8[e]).

You long for us to "put on" our "new nature," and "be renewed" as we "learn to know" you and "become like" you (Colossians 3:10[f]).

Forgive us, Lord, for being so easily distracted by things you have already promised to take care of: "'What will we eat? What will we drink? What will we wear?' These things dominate the thoughts of unbelievers," and you have made it clear that our "heavenly Father already knows" all our "needs" (Matthew 6:31–32[g]). So I leave those worries in your hands right now and ask you will help me to trust you to provide.

Your Word says that those who love you will one day be dressed in "the finest of pure white linen," which "represents the good deeds of" your "holy people" (Revelation 19:8[h]).

I pray she will dress herself in those deeds now, and "put on righteousness" as her "clothing" (Job 29:14).

She can only do this if you help her, Lord Jesus. Please give her grace to "put on" her "new nature, created to be like" you—"truly righteous and holy" (Ephesians 4:24[i]).

You have told us, "Blessed are all who are watching" for you, "who keep their clothing ready" (Revelation 16:15ʲ).

Cover her with your righteousness, Lord! May her life be "hidden with" you in God, so she may one day "appear with" you "in glory" (Colossians 3:3–4)!

a ESV, b NLT, c NLT, d ESV, e NLT, f NLT, g NLT, h NLT, i NLT, j NLT

FATHER'S EYES

"And afterward, I will pour out my Spirit on
all people.
Your sons and daughters will prophesy,
your old men
will dream dreams, your young men will
see visions."

Joel 2:28

Your dreams for my child are far greater than mine, Father.

I have a lifetime in view, but you can see from here to eternity.

I "see" only "dimly" (1 Corinthians 13:12[a]) and my vision for his life is tainted with self and sin.

But your sight is perfect. You see what my child will be ages from now in time beyond time, when you have given him "a new name" (Revelation 2:17[b]) and made him what he was always meant to be.

"What we will be has not yet been made known." You alone know that! "But we know that when Christ appears, we shall be like him" (1 John 3:2).

I praise you for our Savior and the life to come!

Before you return, Lord Jesus, you've given us your Spirit, who makes known to us what "he receives from" you (John 16:15ᶜ).

Your Spirit also "has revealed" to us (1 Corinthians 2:10ᵈ) that the Father has beautiful things planned for those who love him!

I pray that my child will see this and catch a vision of the good you have waiting for him.

Let it captivate his mind and heart, Lord! I pray you will lead him into new heights and depths of understanding how wonderful you are, because "the Spirit searches all things, even the deep things of God" (1 Corinthians 2:10).

I pray he will be caught up in your vision for his life, Father. The world has so many counterfeits; I pray he will have "the mind of Christ" (1 Corinthians 2:16ᵉ) so he may understand your will for him.

Please give him grace to "walk in obedience" to you and "keep" your "commands" so that you "will bless" him (Deuteronomy 30:16) as long as he lives.

And should you bless him with many years, may his vision increase!

When he is older, I pray his eyes will not be fixed on the 'glory days' of his youth. I ask that you will "show" him "your glory" (Exodus 33:18)!

May he "dream dreams" (Joel 2:28) of how good it will be to one day see you "face to face" (Numbers 12:8ᶠ) and live forever in the beauty and peace of your presence.

What better thought could fill his mind than you?

What earthly dream could he long for that could give him more joy than you?

You are "the eternal God" (Romans 16:26[g]), and you alone are "great" and "most worthy of praise" (1 Chronicles 16:25).

You do "not take" your eyes "off the righteous"; you even exalt "them forever" (Job 36:7).

How good you are! How amazingly kind you are to save sinners!

"May those who love your salvation say evermore, 'God is great!'" (Psalm 70:4[h]), and praised forever and ever!

a ESV, b ESV, c NLT, d ESV, e ESV, f NKJV, g ESV, h ESV

"LOVES ME, LOVES ME NOT"

All night long on my bed
I looked for the one my heart loves.

Song of Songs 3:1

Today I pray for the love of my child's life.

I'm not just thinking about the person she will marry. I'm thinking about the one person who can make all the relationships in her life work—you!

Your Word tells us, "Above all else, guard your heart, for everything you do flows from it" (Proverbs 4:23).

How easily are the waters of that spring muddied when we don't let in your love, Lord Jesus! But you promised that "rivers of living water will flow" from the "heart" of "anyone who believes" in you (John 7:38ᵃ).

So, first of all, I pray that you will be the love of my child's life.

I ask that she will not need a man to make her happy; I pray she will find her "heart's desire" (Psalm 20:4ᵇ) in you.

I pray my daughter will be so close to you that she will seek your guidance and blessing in all of the relationships in her life. "The desire of the righteous ends only in good" (Proverbs 11:23[c])!

I ask you to help her choose her relationships wisely.

When she is attracted to someone, I pray that she will be able to reach beyond her human desires and ask, 'Is this what God wants?'

It is a hard thing to pray, "Not my will, but yours, be done" (Luke 22:42[d]). But if she does that, Lord Jesus, she will be following your example.

The human heart is so fickle; it loves and then loves not. But you can "keep" her "heart on the right path" (Proverbs 23:19).

If you live in her and love through her, she will be truly blessed.

"True wisdom" is "found in" you; "counsel and understanding" are yours (Job 12:13[e]). You are the "Wonderful Counselor" (Isaiah 9:6[f])!

If she walks closely with you, she will be protected from making decisions based only on human desire or wisdom.

If it is your desire that she be single, I ask that she will be strong and joyful, doing your work and thinking about "how to please" you (1 Corinthians 7:32[g]).

If it is your desire that she "should marry" (1 Corinthians 7:9), I ask that you will lead her to "a good person" (Proverbs 13:22) who loves you and loves her deeply. May he treat her like "a treasure" (Proverbs 18:22[h])!

If they both love and obey you, you will give them the grace to "submit to one another out of reverence" for you (Ephesians 5:21), so that they will live in your peace.

I also ask that you help them to "remain faithful to one another in marriage" (Hebrews 13:4ⁱ), so they will be protected from the heartache and destruction of sin.

If it is your will, please bless them with children. May they know you and love you too! "Children are a gift" from you (Psalm 127:3ʲ)!

You invented love, and only you can make it work. May she long for you "above all" (John 3:31)!

And, above all, I pray that you will be the one her "heart loves" (Song of Songs 3:1).

a NLT, b ESV, c ESV, d ESV, e NLT, f ESV, g NLT, h NLT, i NLT, j NLT

SO LOVED

"For God so loved the world that he gave
his one and only Son,
that whoever believes in him shall not perish but have eternal life."

John 3:16

Sometimes when I look at my child, I wonder how I could love him more.

I love him so much that it hurts, Father!

And no one understands that better than you.

"This is how" you showed your "love among us." You sent your "one and only Son into the world that we might live through him" (1 John 4:9).

"He personally carried our sins in his body on the cross so that we can be dead to sin and live for what is right." For "by his wounds" we "are healed" (1 Peter 2:24[a]).

You "so loved" us that you "gave" us your "one and only Son" (John 3:16), even when we had "rebelled against you" (Psalm 5:10[b]) and were lost in our sinfulness and self-will.

"So loved" (John 3:16). I love those two words, Father!

We are so loved, and I pray my child will understand that.

I know how imperfect my love is. "When what is perfect comes, the things that are not" fade away (1 Corinthians 13:10ᶜ). Even the love I have for my child is nothing compared to yours!

Oh, how I want him to know the blessing of your love!

I pray that you will use me in any way you desire to share your perfect love with him.

I think of what Mary told the angel you sent to announce Jesus' birth: "I am the Lord's servant" (Luke 1:38).

"I *am* your servant," Lord. Please "give me discernment that I may understand" (Psalm 119:125, italics added) whatever you want me to do.

Since you "so loved us, we also ought to love one another" (1 John 4:11ᵈ). Please give me grace to love him with the love you give.

Human love, even at its best, can only reach so far. But "Your love, LORD, reaches to the heavens," and "your faithfulness to the skies" (Psalm 36:5).

"Your love" for us "is very great. You have rescued" us "from the depths of death" (Psalm 86:13ᵉ), and I want to praise you always for what you have done!

"It is good to praise" you, "O Most High" (Psalm 92:1). "It is good to proclaim your unfailing love in the morning" and "your faithfulness in the evening" (Psalm 92:2ᶠ).

Please help me to love you fully and faithfully so that my child will be drawn to your loving presence through me.

In our world today, there are so many counterfeit notions of what love is; please let my child see the real thing—your love, reflected through me.

There is nothing like your love! "Your love is better than life" (Psalm 63:3)—and stronger than death!

Your love is my child's deepest need.

I pray he will know you have "so loved" him (John 3:16), and love you in return for all of eternity.

HOME

> Praise be to the God and Father of our
> Lord Jesus Christ, who has blessed us in the
> heavenly realms with every spiritual bless-
> ing in Christ.
>
> Ephesians 1:3

Home at last.

That's the single greatest blessing I ask for my child, Father.

I pray that when her "race" is "run" she will have "run in such a way as to get the prize" (1 Corinthians 9:24).

You are our heart's true home. You made us to love you and serve you forever!

I praise you for "the glorious grace" you have "poured out" on those "who belong" to your "dear Son" (Ephesians 1:6ᵃ).

You have already "blessed us in the heavenly realms with every spiritual blessing in Christ" (Ephesians 1:3)!

We're not home yet, but even now you're with us, empowering us with grace and strength that we wouldn't otherwise have—because you give "the Spirit without limit" (John 3:34)!

What a "beautiful inheritance" (Psalm 16:6[b]) you have prepared for those who sincerely follow you! "Whoever believes in the Son has eternal life" (John 3:36[c]).

I pray that my daughter will believe in you and will follow you all the way home, Lord Jesus. Please rescue her from this world "out of the goodness of your love" (Psalm 109:21)!

I ask that you give me grace to "keep on praying" for her as long as I live, so that through my prayers I may help her "live a life worthy" of your "call" (2 Thessalonians 1:11[d]). What better gift could I give her than the cry of my heart for her salvation?

"As for me and my family, we will serve" you (Joshua 24:15[e])!

Your Word promises that "the children of your servants will live in your presence" (Psalm 102:28), and I am your servant, Lord! May she as my child live in you!

You bless "the home of the righteous" (Proverbs 3:33) and I pray ours will be that, a home where we walk by faith "from generation to generation" (Exodus 3:15).

You "gave" your life "to free us from every kind of sin, to cleanse us, and to make us" your "very own people, totally committed" (Titus 2:14[f]).

May she be that! May she remain "true to" you "with all" her heart (Acts 11:23)!

I pray that she will "prove" herself by her "purity," her "understanding," her "patience," her "kindness," by "the Holy Spirit within" her, and by her "sincere love" for you and for others (2 Corinthians 6:6[g]). May you "be honored because of the way" she lives (2 Thessalonians 1:12[h]), Lord Jesus!

Until the day she is home at last, the race done and the battle won, I pray she will "make every effort to be found spotless, blameless and at peace with" you (2 Peter 3:14). May her heart be in heaven before she ever gets there, longing for home and looking forward to you!

a NLT, b ESV, c ESV, d NLT, e NLT, f NLT, g NLT, h NLT

CONCLUSION

Love Beyond Life

For this reason I kneel before the Father,
from whom every family in heaven and on
earth derives its name. I pray that out of
his glorious riches he may strengthen you
with power through his Spirit in your inner
being, so that Christ may dwell in your
hearts through faith.

Ephesians 3:14–17

"Mom, the good news is I've become a Christian."

Sarah looked intently at her son. "And the bad news?"

The story that followed was one no parent hopes to hear. Sarah's son had been caught smuggling drugs in the trunk of his car across state lines. There was little doubt he would be found guilty, and it looked like Robert would go to prison for years.

Sarah had done her best to raise her son to believe in Jesus. Every Sunday of his young life found them at church, but the lure of wealth and the world pulled him to a place Sarah never imagined. Still, she placed Robert in God's hands day by day and loved him through her prayers. After he repented, Sarah still grieved the mistakes he had made, but she was grateful to see a sincere new faith in him.

When the case against Robert was dismissed on a technicality, no one was more surprised than Sarah. And no one was more pleased as her son continued steadfastly in his newfound faith.

It was four decades later that I met Robert. Sarah was celebrating her eighty-first birthday and her children and grandchildren had gathered around her to reminisce. The air was full of laughter as one by one they shared their stories.

When Robert stood to speak he was doing his best to fight back tears. He didn't mention what had happened one summer so many years earlier—there were many in the room who knew nothing about that. To look at him now you might have guessed—rightly—that Robert had been a Sunday school teacher for years and that he loved his mother deeply.

You might have also noticed, from their shared glances, that there seemed to be a special understanding between them, like that of two people who had returned from a long and difficult journey with a story known only to each other. Robert wrapped up his thoughts with his own rendition of a well-known poem, changing only two words in the last line.

> You may have tangible wealth untold;
> Caskets of jewels and coffers of gold.
> Richer than I you can never be—
> I had a mother who prayed for me.

When we give our children the gift of our prayers, we give them a future where hope awaits them in unexpected places. We find that even miracles are possible through the strength of a Savior whose "love is better than life" (Psalm 63:3). And he does "all things well" (Mark 7:37 ESV).

SOURCES

Augustine, Aurelius. *The Confessions of St. Augustine.* Translated by Edward B. Pusey. Oak Harbor, WA: Logos Research Systems, Inc., 1999. Available at Christian Classics Ethereal Library, http://www.ccel.org/ccel/augustine/confess.i.html.

Bennett, Arthur, ed. *The Valley of Vision.* Edinburgh, Scotland: The Banner of Truth Trust, 1975.

Browning, Robert. *Men and Women.* 1898 original edition generated as eBook by Dick Adicks, 2005. Available at Project Gutenberg, http://www.gutenberg.org/cache/epub/17393/pg17393.html.

Chesterton, Gilbert Keith. *A Short History of England.* Available at The Literature Network, http://www.online-literature.com/chesterton/short-history-of-england/.

Cymbala, Jim. *Fresh Wind, Fresh Fire.* Grand Rapids, MI: Zondervan, 1997.

Edwards, Jonathan. *The Works of Jonathan Edwards,* vol. 1. Peabody, MA: Hendrickson Publishers, 1998.

Gillilan, Strickland. "The Reading Mother." Public domain.

Graham, Ruth Bell. *Prodigals and Those Who Love Them.* Grand Rapids, MI: Baker, 1999.

Henderson, Daniel. *Fresh Encounters.* Colorado Springs, CO: NavPress, 2004.

Lewis, Clive Staples. *The Last Battle.* New York, NY: Macmillan Publishing, 1956.

McCasland, David, editor. *The Quotable Oswald Chambers.* Grand Rapids, MI: Discovery House Publishers, 2008.

Metaxas, Eric. *Bonhoeffer.* Nashville, TN: Thomas Nelson, 2010.

Morgan, Robert J. *Moments for Families with Prodigals.* Colorado Springs, CO: Navpress, 2003.

Newton, John. *The Life and Spirituality of John Newton*, introduction by D. Bruce Hindmarsh. Vancouver, B.C.: Regent College Publishing, 2003.

Newton, John, and William Cowper. *Olney Hymns.* London: W. Oliver, 1797.

Nightengale, Bob. "Pastor Strawberry Says True Calling Ahead, Not Baseball," *USA Today*, July 12, 2013. Available at http://www.usatoday.com/story/sports/mlb/2013/07/11/darryl-strawberry-tracy-strawberry-ministries-new-york-mets-drugs/2509921/.

Ryle, J.C. "Are You Fighting?" Available at SermonIndex
.net, www.sermonindex.net/modules/articles/index.php
?view=article&aid=2331.

Spurgeon, Charles Haddon. *The C. H. Spurgeon Collection.*
Rio, WI: Ages Software, 1998–2001.

INDEX

NOTE TO THE READER

The publisher invites you to share your response to the message of this book by writing Discovery House Publishers, P.O. Box 3566, Grand Rapids, MI 49501, U.S.A. For information about other Discovery House books, music, or DVDs, contact us at the same address or call 1-800-653-8333. Find us on the Internet at dhp.org or send e-mail to books@dhp.org.

ABOUT THE AUTHOR

Dr. James Banks's books have encouraged many people to pray. He is the author of *The Lost Art of Praying Together*, *Prayers for Prodigals*, *Praying the Prayers of the Bible*, *The Praying the Prayers of the Bible Perpetual Calendar*, and *Let's Pray* (Discovery Series). James and his wife, Cari, have been married thirty years and make their home in Durham, North Carolina, where James is the founding pastor of Peace Church. They have two adult children. James is a much-loved speaker at conferences, retreats, churches, and special events. For more information about hosting an event with James, please visit JamesBanks.org.